No Peace Without Justice

For Liesel
My inspiration

Beth

The
Unfinished
Feminist

Beth Glick-Rieman

Arc Light Books
Oakland, California

The Unfinished Feminist

ISBN: 978-1939353122
1. Woman's Rights. 2. Biography. I. Title.

Published in the United States by
Arc Light Books in Oakland, California
www.arclightbooks.com • publisher@arclightbooks.com

Cover photo courtesy of Women's Empowerment International
Design and publishing support by Jan Camp, jan.camp@ymail.com

Other Books by Beth Glick-Rieman

Peace Train to Beijing and Beyond

Peggy, I May Not Have the Summer

Opening Your Heart

Write For Your Life

For my mother, Effie Iwilla Evers Glick,
and my father, John Titus

I FIRST MET BETH GLICK-RIEMAN *when she was 91 and leading a personal-development writing group. Though petite, she was strong, clear, and independent—an amazing role model, and remarkably still driving her own car. There was no question of her inner strength, determination, and innate leadership.*

We became friends around the making of this book. Beth had overcome the theft of her original manuscript when burglars stole a laptop with the only copy. Though resolved to rewrite the book in its entirety, her eyesight began to fail. I found myself privileged to work with her, an accomplished author, in the revisions and final story telling that completed this book.

—Nelline Kowbel

Nelline and Beth—Beth's first "Selfie"

CONTENTS

THANKS

As I celebrate bringing this life story to a momentary pause, and give it to an audience interested in the lives of this century's women, I am filled with gratitude for those who have made it possible.

Write For Your Life, my inspirational and committed writing group, kept me anchored to the task. Each one of you played a part in keeping me faithful to the dream. Without Nelline's encouragement and expertise at the computer I would have surely thrown the document to the winds many times. Without Jan Camp's expertise and generosity as a publisher this book would never have come into being.

My children and their spouses believed I had something that needed to be said at my time in history.

Friends without number have contributed to the content— and stand waiting to read what I have to say.

My beloved parents gave me a legacy of truth and knowledge, and belief in myself. All of these activated the spirit and creativity within me. Without them I could never have fulfilled the dream of being a writer.

FOREWORD

Tamalpais in the Marin Headlands of California and majestic Massanutten Peak in the luscious green Shenandoah Valley of Virginia are bookends that hold together the cow paths, hiking trails, freeways and all manner of roads that comprise the lifetime journey of one woman of the twentieth century. She was called by many "a radical feminist," "a bra burner," and, by some unenlightened men, "a man hater."

The decades, nine plus of them, have stacked one upon another, inexorably, like a pile of China plates at the ready to hold the gourmet meal waiting to be served. Nine decades and more! A full and remarkable life. MINE!

One

BEFORE THE BEGINNING

John Titus and Effie Iwilla Evers Glick,
Beth's father and mother

There is really no way to find "the beginning." The planet Earth, with all its immense complexities of peoples, cultures, religions, educational systems, languages, music, governments, sciences, warmongering and peacemaking, sports, colors, and entertainment, was centuries in progress long before I screamed my lusty entrance into the world of air. My forebears had fled their native countries to escape religious persecution. Emigrating from Germany, England and Scotland, they settled themselves as farmers in the lush countryside of the Shenandoah Valley of Virginia. There were eight or so generations of Glicks, dominated by Elizabeths and Johns and Joes before me. There were Zimmermans and Evers, Millers and Clines with their Daniel (Bud), William, Lydia and their own Elizabeth Alice called Lizzie. From these unknown generations emerged Joseph Miller Glick and Diana Miller Glick, on my paternal side, and Daniel (Bud) Evers (long e) who claimed Elizabeth Cline as his wife, and who together became my maternal grandparents. The Glick and Evers families were well known and highly respected in the Valley. John Titus was number five of the ten Glick children of five boys and five girls. Effie Iwilla was number one of five Evers children, all girls. John and Effie married on the long, pillared porch of the Evers' farmhouse on June 15, 1915 and became my beloved parents.

Dozens more of these lifetimes, long gone, are only initials on my vintage, satin quilt. I know so little of the conditions of their lives, the facts of their daily living, the struggles, joys, disappointments, triumphs and sorrows, the achievements and failures. I do know that when they left their native lands, it was because they were seeking a place where they could worship according to the dictates of their own conscience. They wanted to be free of the heavy doctrinal hand of the ecclesiastical establishment of the day.

I know that they were a unique sort, whose motto was "live simply so that others may simply live." I know they wanted to live peaceably with all, that they believed they were "their brother's keeper," that "to whom much is given, much is required." I know they had a moral code that denied the use of alcohol, the playing of cards, the wearing of any form of jewelry. A code that required strict adherence to the Biblical Ten Commandments: No other God but the Hebrew Jahweh; no taking the Lord's name in vain; no making graven images and bowing down to them. No work on Sunday; no coveting your neighbor's wife or anything that is your neighbor's; do not kill; do not commit adultery; do not steal; honor your father and mother; remember the Sabbath Day to keep it holy; do not bear false witness against your neighbor.[1]

I know these strange people loved music and often gathered for "hymn-sings" in the church or at each others' homes. I know they loved nature and believed "The earth is the Lord's and the fullness thereof, the world and they that dwell therein."[2]

I know these people were hard-working, humble, persevering, dedicated to God and to making peace on earth. I know I was born into a goodly heritage.

Daddy was a southern gentleman. He had been into his studies for the PhD at Northwestern University in Elgin, Illinois when he married Mama. When she became pregnant a couple months later, he left the university, just short of his goal of a PhD, and they settled in the home country near Bridgewater, Virginia, into the tasks of raising a family.

Daddy loved learning. He was a debater; gave it up with

regret. He became the teacher/principal of the village school of Centerville, to which we kids all went.

He always showed deep respect of Mama's parents and his own. A tender memory I treasure is of walking with Daddy as he approached their graves, pausing with his hand over his heart, then, tipping his black Fedora; wordlessly moving nearer the graves, as if in reverent memory and prayer.

Mama also was educated with a Bachelor of English Degree, which was rare for women in those days. It qualified her to teach elementary school, but twelve pregnancies and childbirths intervened.

Mama was an artist, a painter, who gave up her chosen career for the sake of being a full-time homemaker, raising twelve kids. She wanted to be a missionary in a foreign field, but she was turned down by the elders in charge because she was "too frail." She smiled ruefully as she told the story: "They said I was too frail to withstand the rigors of missionary life, so I stayed home, married John Glick, gave birth and raised twelve babies!"

Many years later, I wanted to get her to reach for that artist dream again, and gave her a complete set of artist's tools. A couple weeks later, she told me thanks, but that she could not use them: "My fingers are too stiff from washing too many baby diapers." I never heard her express any regret, but I still feel cheated at the loss of her dream.

Mama was also an avid reader and Bible scholar. She taught Sunday School for many years and was actively engaged in the life of the community. Deaths or tragedy in a neighboring family always meant Mama was there for a visit, with a casserole and an empathetic listening ear.

To locate one tiny drop, my lifetime, in the ongoing flood-waters of human history, and to discern the impact of that life on its own time, is a formidable, perhaps impossible, task. My brother Wayne, in derision, calls it "navel-gazing." I, on the other hand, with the vantage point of all these decades of living believe that each lifetime has rich gifts to give to its peers and descendants. If we are willing to take the effort to ferret out the spiritual meaning of our life journey, those who come after might have a needed perspective on their own living. I believe that my lifetime is no exception. Furthermore, to undertake to discover those gifts and meanings is to feast on the goodness of my life, for which I am profoundly grateful.

As a young child I sang,

Little drops of water, little grains of sand,
Make the mighty ocean and the pleasant land.
Little deeds of kindness, little words of love,
Make the earth an Eden, like the heaven above.

Perhaps my writing this book will give some reader the courage to contribute to "making the earth an Eden" by facing into their own, challenging trials with hope and joy. That's what reading Helen Keller's *Story of My Life* did for me.

She Has Done What She Could

—Matthew 26:10b KJV

Two

THE THUNDEROUS, TENDER TWENTIES

I'm thinking about time as an embryo
within the embryo within the accident
or peak of my parents' desires
to create a life, to give birth
to ME.[3]

It was a cold, mid-winter night in January, 1922 when Effie Iwilla Evers and John Titus Glick, now the parents of four boys, snuggled and made love. Many years later Mama told me that the act of sex was not enjoyable to her, but that she believed it was the duty of the wife to let it happen. She believed sex was designed to satisfy the male and make babies.

The X's and Y's arranged themselves into girl shape, and on October 2, I screamed my lusty entrance into the world of air. I think that being born to those two was the best thing that ever happened to me.

I was born into that nest full of boys with writhing penises, four of them: Wendell, Victor, John Jr. and Wayne. I was pre-destined to become a radical feminist.

It was 1922, a time of unrest, or, as one writer put it, "a time of fads, fashions, and mass lunacy."

Five years earlier, in 1917, President Woodrow Wilson had led the nation into and through the first World War. In an effort to build "an enduring peace," in 1918 he had asked Congress to establish "a general association of nations—affording mutual guarantees of political independence and territorial integrity to great and small states alike." He presented to the Senate the Treaty of Versailles, which contained the Covenant of The League of Nations, the precursor of our United Nations.

The year before I was in gestation, 1921, Warren G. Harding, a staunch Republican, had won the presidency, declaring that "America's present need is not heroics, but healing, not nostrums but normalcy, not revolution but restoration." With Congress, he slashed taxes and eliminated wartime controls. To the adult population, it seemed that the postwar depression was giving way and prosperity was abounding. Then, suddenly, and some say mysteriously, President Harding died of a heart attack, and Calvin Coolidge moved into the White House.

Every institution and system of society was being bombarded with change. My valiant foremothers, after great struggle, abuse and sacrifice, and to whom I am eternally grateful, were basking in the glow of gaining women's suffrage. African American jazz kept white feet, as well as black, pounding to the beat.

The assumption of the absolute truth of "the way things are," having been undergirded for years by religion, education, the home, the public/political sphere, was no longer true. It was being challenged everywhere in those same organizations and structures, both in the nation and on the global scene.

The notion that our Big Island was not the center of the earth, but rather one small territory in a vast collection of nations, all connected and interdependent, was taking root. Black and white movies elicited "ooo"s and "ahhh"s in theaters across the nation. Flamboyant dancers swayed to the Charleston. It was the time of flappers and pin striped suits, the Model T and the automobile revolution. The stock market was booming and credit was easy. Folk singers and vaudeville troops entertained thousands with slapstick humor and evident disregard for chaotic Wall Street and uneasy Main Street. Chautauqua teams traveled the nation providing music and lectures that enriched the cultural life of communities far and near.

The First World War had deadened the joy and security of thousands of families. People sought refuge and comfort in overflowing churches. The age-old conflict between religion and science sparked into flame in the ludicrous Scopes Trial, the "Monkey Trial," where orthodox Christianity in the person of William Jennings Bryan sparred with Clarence Darrow, an ardent evolutionist who was determined to keep religion out of the public schools. As a small child, I remember Daddy talking about this struggle over mealtimes.

At birth, as #5, first girl, I was ensconced and isolated in my secure family nest in the Church of the Brethren parsonage in that little town of Timberville, in the heart of the shimmering Shenandoah Valley.

I was a "preacher's kid." Daddy was the pastor of the little village Church of the Brethren in our town.

I learned early on that being born female was somehow not as good as being born male. Having a penis meant you could be the leader in our kid games and choose who would be on your side. You would never have to be the last chosen, which was almost always my fate. Having a penis meant privilege, that the playing ground was not equal, that I could never win in the peeing contests my brothers cooked up. I didn't know then that the deck was stacked against me at my birth. I tried hard to win, but never did.

Daddy was the decision maker in the home, the breadwinner, the money manager, the "spiritual head of the house." Mama presided over the home, the kitchen, the children. The boys could climb trees anytime they wanted. I had to wear dresses and sit properly with legs together and grow up to "be a lady." When Mama reprimanded me for climbing trees, and I asked why the boys could, she said: "The boys will look up under your dress and see your underwear." Girls did not wear pants in those days, at least not in my family. Mama had her reasons. They made no sense to me. "So what's the big deal?" I thought. But I got the message: girls are different than boys, and that means boys can do things girls cannot do. Later on, I would call that reality a double standard, a lack of privilege. I can still hear Mama's scolding voice, "Elizabeth, will you ever grow up to be a lady?"

That "privileged status" also was played out by Mama and Daddy. It seemed to me that Mama had to get Daddy's permission for everything she wanted to do, even though he seemed proud of her being "spunky from the git-go."

Daddy loved to tell the story of when as a young man, he worked for her father in the only little store in town, Centerville General. One day Effie was sent to the store from the big colonial brick house where they lived about a mile away, to get kindling, to ask John to chop it fine. When he did so and presented it to her, she said, "That's not fine enough. Do it over." He did it over. He was nearly eleven years her senior. He declared to me that it was at that moment that he thought to himself, "I'm going to wait till that girl grows up and marry her!" He also declared that when that time came, he had to "beat out" several admirers who had the same thing in mind: Howard and Aubrey were the most ardent.

"But I got the prize," Daddy would say exultantly, and you got her for a mother."

He always treated her with the greatest respect. In a day when the man was considered to be "the spiritual head" of the family, he often said "your mother is far more spiritual than I."

I was born at home with Dr. Vaughn attending Mama. There was no such thing as midwives. Home births were common; money was scarce; and hospital births were expensive. Daddy's meager salary as pastor of the little church in that village did not even cover the basic needs of the growing family. The church folks, out of either generosity or guilt, supplemented his salary with "missionary barrels" and "poundings." Every six months or so, one of the church members who had a truck would appear with piles of used clothing and staples like flour, sugar, rice, potatoes, canned goods. I loved getting a second-hand blue dress when I was five. At the time, I had no aware-ness of the vast inequities in the distribution of wealth in our society, a continuing disgrace to this day, only worse.

Mama was a full-time homemaker without salary. She cooked and cleaned, washed and ironed with black flatirons heated on the kitchen cook stove. She nursed babies and changed thou-sands of diapers, (not disposable) during her nine years of pregnancy and infant care. That's the way it was.

Being the first girl after four boys, with whom I spent a lot of energy and time in those early years trying to be included was a mixed bag. From Daddy I often heard the story of Brother Baugher's visit, when Daddy put me up on the dining room table at age two and said to the visiting minister, "Isn't she a dandy?"

Mama and Daddy were kind parents. And firm. They were able to live by their own principles of child raising even in the face of criticism from parishioners who thought they knew better. There was the apple butter story Daddy told Mama one day after the church service. It seems that the Glick kids had been unseemly unruly, and irreverent after the service by running in the sanctuary. Brother Zigler had informed Daddy that he should do as Brother Hoover did with his children, have them sit on the back steps eating apple butter bread. When he told Mama this story, she responded with her typical asperity: "Our children are allowed to be children. When those Hoover kids grow up, they'll still be sitting on the back steps eating apple butter bread!"

I am increasingly thankful for having been born into a family that considers education and higher learning to be central to living a good life. Even as a small child, I longed for the day when I could go to school with the boys. At age six, that day finally came. My heart was racing as we left home to walk the two blocks up the hill to the square, brick, mysterious schoolhouse. My oldest brother, Wendell, was assigned the task of getting me to the proper place. In those days there was no kindergarten; there were six years of elementary school and four years of high school, a total of ten.

When he left me for his own classroom and I found myself in the schoolyard with lots of STRANGE kids my age, I felt anxious, awkward and very excited.

E. Lizzie Trussel, austere and commanding in her black, floor length outfit, complete with ruler in hand, appeared and took charge. I was literally scared out of my mind. At the bell in the schoolyard, we arranged ourselves, boys in one line, girls in another, then marched into the schoolroom and took assigned brown, lidded desks in rows alphabetized according to the first letter of our last name. The fact that mine was "G" put me in the very last desk on the first row. I felt very grown-up, and very uneasy at the same time. Having my very own desk was a thrill.

I held E. Lizzie in awe that whole first year. She was a strict, no-nonsense disciplinarian. I hated her sometimes, like when Frank peed in his pants, and was punished by being required to stand, face to the wall, in front of the whole class. I thought she was cruel and unfair. I used to wonder why she didn't call on me to answer her questions instead of on the "dumb" kids who didn't even have their hands up. Looking back now, I realize that she took seriously what she understood a good teacher to be. I did learn the basics: reading, writing and arithmetic, and for that I thank you, E. Lizzie.

I'm sure I was a nuisance to those "big kids," as we called my four older brothers. And they did often gang up on me.

One day I overheard Wendell and Victor talking about me:

Wendell: Girls are sissies. She won't do it.

Victor: Let's ask her. I think she will.

Wendell: I bet she won't.

Victor: I bet she will.

A while later, those two, along with Junior (Johnnie was called "Junior" or "Pune" until he was in his teens) and Wayne invited me to play a game with them. There was a car-shed in back of the parsonage. It had a slanted roof, very high off the ground. How we got up on that roof I'll never know, but we lined up by age, from the highest point. Wendell was nearest to the bottom. The game was to reach the lowest point when our turn came, and from there jump to the ground. Wendell jumped first. Then Vic. Junior next; then Wayne. I became more scared with every jump. By the time my turn came, I was terrified, but there was no way I was ever going to disappoint Vic. Just as I jumped, Mama came out of the house and realized what was going on. She screamed, scolding the boys severely, which I enjoyed immensely! But the deed was done. At seven I thought I was not injured and it felt good to have Mama defend me. Years later, in diagnosing severe menstrual cramps in my teens, Dr. Miller told me I had a prolapsed uterus. Thanks, big kids. It was the first of many pranks my brothers played to tantalize me as "girl."

My brothers seemed to me to keep busy thinking up ways to tantalize me. They would watch for the time when Mama was going to put me to bed. Then, without her knowing, they would crawl in under my bed and lie in wait silently for her to leave the room. Just as I was about to drop off to sleep, they would growl and curve their backs to lift up on the mattress from below. By the time my terrified scream for Mama brought her to my rescue, they had scrambled out into the yard far from the scene of the crime, leaving Mama to wonder what on earth had caused my terror as she calmed me one more time.

We lived two blocks up the hill from the Minnichs, and Frank and I became good playmates. He was nine when I was seven. One day at his house he suggested that we go up to the attic to play.

"Let's play doctor," he said when we were alone. Young, naive and innocent as I was, I agreed.

"I'll be the doctor and you be the patient," he said, and asked me to take off my panties and lie down on an old couch there.

"Open your legs," he said. Unsuspecting, I did as he told me. In pure innocence, (I felt no sense of wrongdoing) as he began to inspect and touch my genitals. At that moment, Mama somehow appeared, looking for me. Her look of horror and her stern reprimand have stayed with me all my life. In an instant my innocence was turned to shame. I had done something terribly wrong and it had to do with my being a girl. I didn't even know what it was! I only knew that I was not allowed to play with Frank ever again. I felt ashamed of myself whenever I saw him. I carried that shame into my adulthood and even my marriage. Therapy helped.

I was seven years old in the spring of 1930, when the stark reality of death and sorrow shook the safe haven of security and certainty of all my years before. It was morning, and I was in the kitchen of the parsonage with Mama. The big brown crank telephone on the well rattled with intensity. Mama put the long, black receiver to her ear, and, an instant later, her voice took on an air of hushed sadness. "Oh, when did it happen? Listening. Then, "Thanks for calling. We will come right away."

She turned to me. "Elizabeth, go over to the church and tell Daddy to come home right away."

Minutes later, as he walked toward her with an anxious look, tears streamed down her face. "Papa died this morning." Daddy took her in his arms, and they wept together.

My world tilted on its axis. It took only a moment for me to know that life would never again be the same. Daddy and Mama crying? Only children cry. Parents are different. Dying? What does that mean? In the blink of an eye, everything changed, was somehow confusing, different.

I begged to go along on the trip to Grandfather Evers' farm twenty-five miles away. I thought Mama and Daddy sensed my need to be with them, so granted my wish. Now I know that they took me along because all the oldest girls in the families of each daughter of Grandfather Evers were to be "flower girls" during the funeral service.

At the farm, my child mind was truly shaken. I followed Mama upstairs to the bedroom where my four aunts, her sisters, had gone apart and taken refuge. All of them were weeping, too. I wondered where Grandfather was, why he didn't come to say hello like he always did. Everything was strangely different,

The next day, Mama took me into the parlor to see Grandfather lying in his satin-lined coffin. With a shock I saw that this ghostly-looking man was not my jolly Grandfather Evers, not at all like I remembered him. I touched his hand. It was clammy, white, cold, weird, very still. It was all so scary.

Several days later, I was one of the five first cousin girls who met before the service began and were each given a huge bouquet to carry after the eight men, pallbearers, who carried the coffin to the front of the church, and opened the lid for all the people to see during the service. We flower girls then placed our bouquets on either side, and sat facing the coffin. People were crying everywhere. Little muffled sobs.

As the service began, the people began to sing. Their voices rang out clear and strong:

> *O happy day that fixed my choice*
> *On thee, my Savior and my God*
> *Well may this glowing heart rejoice*
> *And spread its raptures all abroad.*
>
> *Happy Day! Happy Day!*
> *When Jesus washed my sins away.*
> *He taught me how to watch and pray,*
> *And live rejoicing every day,*
>
> *Happy Day! Happy Day!*
> *When Jesus washed my sins away.*

I felt more confused, and now, angry. It made no sense to me that we were singing about being happy, when my grandfather was dead and everybody was crying and sad. I whispered to Mama, "Why did they have to choose that hymn, Mama?" She shushed me.

After the service, while Grandfather still lay in the open coffin in the front of the church, the people filed by, one by one, past that shockingly still body. Then they continued solemnly and silently out of the church to the cemetery about fifty yards from the building. We flower girls picked up our bouquets and stood aside as the pallbearers came forward and closed the casket. We followed them in a solemn procession outside to where the people had gathered in the cemetery. There, we joined them around a big hole in the ground beside a tall gravestone marked "Elizabeth Alice Cline Evers."

I knew that was my Grandmother Evers' grave because Mama had taken me with her when she placed a bouquet of purple iris there on Mother's Day long ago. I remembered Mama's tears and how special I felt when she took my hand and said ever so sadly, "She died in childbirth when I was only 15 years old. I'm glad we gave you her name." I felt very close to Mama that day. And now we were about to bury her father!

The pallbearers lowered the casket halfway down into the hole, and shoveled a few mounds of earth on it. Then they stood aside as we placed the flowers all around it. The minister said solemnly "Ashes to ashes; dust to dust." They lowered the casket into the ground and began to fill the hole with huge mounds of dirt piled onto the casket. I felt a sense of horror, realizing that I would never see my grandfather again. It was more than I could bear. I broke into sobs. I ran to Mama and hid my face in her skirt. She patted me gently on the head.

What I did not know at that time was that my own life would be pulled up from the roots and be forever changed by the juxtaposition of this death and my dawning sexuality. Everything seemed new and scary; I was uneasy, afraid.

A short few months later Daddy and Mama told us kids that they had bought Grandfather Evers' farm and the family would be moving away from Timberville to live every day on the farm. Daddy would give up his chosen profession as paid minister and become a farmer and a respected community elder. He was available to anyone in times of crisis. Almost immediately, plans and packing took the place of my well-ordered, secure days. The big move came in September, just before the opening of the school year, and I would be attending Centerville Elementary. Though I felt comfort and the support of the family, this big transition was an uneasy time for me.

Coming, as it did, on the heels of the stock market crash of the year before, which had put millions of everyday Americans into an era of uneasiness, struggle, pain, misery, tumultuous change and deprivation, I felt as if the whole world were shaking and uneasy.

I had not known, when the call came that put Mama in tears, that it meant a major move of the family from the village of Timberville to the farm near Centerville. I did not know that the move meant I was entering a whole new culture, with many farm chores, bus rides to school, the countryside and woods as playground, horses and cows named Maude and Prince. Sundays around the piano singing hymns and folk melodies like "Seeing Nellie Home" and "Old Black Joe" seemed to be the only thing that continued as before.

Three

THE TURBULENT, TROUBLED THIRTIES

All of us, everywhere in the world, from the day
we're born, are indoctrinated with arbitrary rules
of behavior, distorted images of reality, and value
systems that demand that we pretend to be less than we
are. Cultural stems force living things into boxes.[4]

The decade of the thirties moved into my life like ocean waves crashing on the towering rocks of the Oregon shoreline. All my naive assumptions and presumptions were blown to smithereens, inside the family and outside in the culture.

The stock market crash of 1929 had ushered in the Great Depression which launched millions of everyday Americans into an era of uneasiness, tumultuous change and deprivation.

Poverty was on the rise; bankruptcies and homelessness became common. Many men who could not feed their families sought solace in alcohol; families were torn apart. Everywhere people were suffering.

Looking back now, I hear the loose shutters clanging in the night on that old brick farmhouse of my childhood, to which we had moved. Sundays were special. It was "the Lord's Day" and no one worked, except Mama of course and Daddy, and a kid or two to milk the cows, feed the pigs, and gather eggs from hens squawking in their nests.

Round about that time the government put into effect the Rural Electrification Program and Wendell did the wiring. I shall never forget that moment when we clicked a button and a room was filled—flooded—with light. Unbelievable! No more smoking coal oil lampshades to clean. No more lanterns or candles needed!

In summer we kids scattered to the turkey field and picked up sides for a game of softball. The older boys headed the teams. I, being a girl, was always picked last. It's "the way we do it," they'd say when I protested.

In winter we shivered around the old potbellied black, barrel-shaped wood stove, trying to warm one side after the other, picking on each other in the process. Huge dishpans of popcorn helped ease the tension. For supper on Sundays, we could each have one-fourth of an apple pie of the twelve or fourteen Mama had labored to bake on Saturday. Pie was all the supper there was, and I made it last by chewing each bite twenty times, as Daddy suggested.

I took playtime for granted. I never knew what it was like to be without a playmate. In the absence of store bought games, we kids made up our own or borrowed from other kids. Jump rope, Jacks. Hide and Seek. On warm summer evenings we competed to see who could catch the most fireflies. We used jars with slotted tops. When it got dark, part of the game was to count them, see who got the most, and let them go.

When it got warm enough in the spring, we played "Mother, May I?" or Hopscotch (if we could find chalk) on the long, white-columned porch that circled two sides of the house. Or Margaret (Mickie) and I built playhouses on the grass up near the wagon shed, or in the dusty cubbyholes inside it. We made rooms with sticks and stones and pretended to be Mama's sisters, Aunt Carrie and Aunt Sada. We visited each other often, had babies, diapered them. Sticks were chairs and brooms and silverware; old license plates were dishes. We actually nibbled at our mud pies and thought they were delicious. Make-believe was real; our imagination knew no bounds. We were happy in those days. For me, life was simple, untroubled, relatively free of anxiety. I had absolutely no awareness that all around us, " the Great Depression" was wreaking havoc in the lives of millions of parents and children. I only knew that we had no money, that every hard-earned penny had to be sent to "The Land Bank of Baltimore."

Strange to think it was a secure early childhood when there was not a penny or a nickel anywhere to be seen.

We moved in September 1930, a month before the opening of Centerville School. I was in third grade, and my teacher would be Miss Beulah Rusmisle.

Scarcely had I adjusted to being a farm girl far out in the country then I found myself in a wilderness of events that were terribly troubling and confusing. In 1931, at age nine, having been told nothing about menstruation, I began to bleed. I thought I was dying. I knew that this would make Mama and Daddy very sad, so I didn't tell them what was happening. A day later, when Mama discovered blood on my bloomers, she took me aside and we had a talk that went something like this:

Mama: Elizabeth, why didn't you tell me you were bleeding?

Elizabeth: I thought it would worry you, Mama.

Mama: No, it wouldn't have worried me, because it happens to all girls. It's called "the curse." Sometimes girls say they've "fallen off the roof." From now on, it will happen to you once a month. It means that your body is getting ready to have babies. Come with me and we'll make some pads out of an old sheet that you'll need to wear when it happens.

She took me down the hill to the building we called "the washhouse." She pointed out a big, tin washtub and said, "You will need to put the bloody rags to soak in cold water until you stop bleeding and then wash them in hot soapy water, rinse them and put them to dry on this clothesline.

"Don't ever mention this to the boys. It's none of their business, and I don't want them to tease you."

I was relieved, and disgusted. What a nuisance it was. I didn't understand at all the connection between this ugly thing and having babies, which I thought was what I wanted to do when I grew up. How ignorant I was of the facts of life in those days. And I felt somehow guilty of Mama's obvious distress over the whole matter. Being a girl was not fun any more.

During that next year, my breasts developed and I became so buxom that Mama made "bodies" out of unbleached muslin that I had to wear tight over my chest to the point that it hurt. I don't know if there were bras at that time, but the message I got was "Your breasts are too large; hide them."

At one point, Johnnie, always the tease, took me on a walk beside the creek and said "You are getting to look really weird. Your chest is sloppy big, and your hair is growing into your eyes. When you grow up, the only thing you'll be able to do is be one of those crazy freaks in the circus that people pay money to look at."

For months after that I used a ruler to measure the distance between my eyes and my hairline, thinking he was right. I trusted and believed those older brothers.

I was terribly naive all through my teens. I got a steady diet of innuendos of female inferiority and male superiority from my brothers, however unintended. It was in the very air I breathed.

Living by the rules was an absolute given. A violation was not tolerated. It brought consequences. The only spanking I can remember was a result of brothers Wayne, Don and I having jumped into the tempting wheat bin, an absolute NO, NO! Daddy and Mama had gone into town, which they rarely did together. We figured they would never know, that we'd get out before they got back. We made up this game, seeing who could put the most wheat grains in our ears and noses. We were at it when suddenly Daddy appeared and caught us. The tone of his voice alerted us to the fact that this was no small transgression: "We will have to go to have Dr. Miller check you out. When we get back, it's the woodshed."

We got it. Going to the doctor meant spending money. It was done only in dire emergencies. Disobeying the rules brought punishment. We were guilty and deserved whatever punishment Daddy decided to mete out.

After our visit to Dr. Miller, we all meekly followed Daddy to the woodshed.

The boys got it first, and they howled appropriately. Then it was my turn. When Daddy tapped me ever so lightly with the old, splintery wood slab, I screamed as if he had nearly killed me. It's the only time he ever laid a hand on me except in caress. Looking back, I am sure it hurt Daddy more than it did me.

Because Daddy was the Elder of the church, he was responsible for planning the yearly two-week revival meeting to "save souls for Christ." I was one of those souls. When I was nine, Brother Guy West, who was known as "a hellfire and brimstone" evangelist, was Daddy's choice for that ritual in Summit Church where we attended. One night, Brother West spoke directly to me, I had become "convicted of sin" because I hated my brothers for teasing me about my being born a girl, and therefore was somehow inferior to them. That night Brother West had preached about hell. Raising his voice, he shouted, "You are neither hot nor cold, but you are lukewarm, and I will spew thee out of my mouth, saith the Lord."

I had trouble sleeping that night. I knew it made me a sinner to feel hate toward my brothers. So the next night when "the invitation" was given to "come forward" and confess my sins. I got up because I was terrified at the thought of burning in hellfire. I walked to Brother West who shook my hand, and invited me to join others who would be baptized soon after the meeting ended.

A few days later, we all gathered with Daddy, on the banks of "the Glade," a little stream that ran through our farm. I was dressed in a pure white cotton dress for the occasion. When my turn came, I waded into the creek into the waiting arms of Daddy. He asked me to kneel. Then, dipped me under the water, and intoned in a serious voice, "In the name of the Father"; dipped me under a second time, "And of the Son "dipped me a third time, "And of the Holy Ghost." He then put both hands on my head and prayed this prayer: "Our Heavenly Father, we give thanks for this soul who has chosen to live her life for Jesus. Forgive all her sins and make her to be white as snow.

May her name be inscribed in the Lamb's Book of Life. And may she be blessed forevermore."

I came out of the creek, shivering and shaking; into the arms of Mama who wrapped me in a long white towel. I was comforted and relieved that I was now saved from the flames of eternal hell.

My relief was short-lived, however. A couple days later, the boys teased me again and I hated them as before. But I had done what I could to be saved. Why had it not worked for me? I wondered. Oh well, they were the guilty ones, anyway. And I had done what I could.

A memory that stands out for me during garden and canning season, is of Mama sitting with bushels of beans, tomatoes, apples or ears of corn on the floor beside her, with a dishpan in her lap that held the harvest and an open book, propped up in the dishpan, so she could read while snapping, cutting, peeling, to ready things for the cooker.

She was diligent in knowing what we kids were reading from the library. She used Bible stories to teach us the life lessons she wanted us to know. When she wanted me to be willing to sit with the baby until sleep came, she told me the story of Miriam and how she watched over her baby brother, Moses, in the bulrushes. To teach me to be brave and strong, she told the story of Daniel in the Lion's Den. She was a consummate storyteller, and a prodigious worker, canning hundreds of quarts and half-gallons of food in a single season. She worked rings around me, putting enough food on the table to feed fourteen hungry people three times a day.

It took a lot of food to feed twelve growing kids and their parents. There was no such thing as being "vegetarian" in those days. Daddy was known in the community as the top butcher. The neighbors always called on him to be at their butchering because he knew just how to cut and trim the meat. His knife blades scared me to death. During butchering season, I often had this horrifying dream that he was using those knives on us kids for misbehaving. It was an "off the wall" dream, very real, though I don't remember ever being afraid of Daddy.

Our butchering day came in the summer when we kids were out of school. Each one of us was given a task to complete. When the pigs had been killed, they were loaded onto the wagon bed and pulled by Prince or King down the hill to the springhouse. I came on the scene after they had been dipped in scalding water and hoisted onto tripods by their hind legs, bare as the day they were born, gutted and ready for Daddy's knives.

My job was to take the dishpan of entrails into the springhouse and scrape them clean and ready for the sausage grinder. I hated that job. It was stinky, terribly yucky, and Mama was a stern boss to be sure I did it right. I felt sorry for the pigs. But when the organs were cooked and we could have a taste of heart or liver, I was right in there getting my share. Neighbors were thought to say, "Those Glicks eat everything but the squeal." We made pickled pigs' feet. We had "pudding" made by grinding up all the organs together. We had it with hominy for breakfast all winter. We could count on eggs with sausage and bacon as long as it lasted. But the lungs? Mama called them "the lights." Somehow, Mama just couldn't cross that line.

In November of 1932, just after I had turned ten, Daddy had chosen "Brother Byrd," a well-known and respected pastor of West Virginia, to be the speaker at our annual revival. Fourteen nights in a row, we went to hear him "preach the gospel."

It was expected that the visiting minister would be hosted in our home. It didn't seem to matter that Mama was already caring for fourteen people, including three new babies born in 1930, '31 and '32.

One day, Brother Byrd asked me to go for a walk with him around the farm. We headed for the cornfield quite away from the house and at a place well hidden, he suggested that we sit down and rest awhile. He said, "Don't tell anybody what we do on our walks together. Let's keep it our secret."

Then he came close to me, pulled up my dress, took down my panties, and started to touch me like Frank had done. I was terrified. The "wrongness" of it made me jump up and run for the house. I hid in my room, shaking and unnerved by it all. The next day, in Daddy's presence, Brother Byrd asked me again to go for a walk.

I said "No I don't want to go. I have to do my homework." Unknowingly, Daddy intervened. "Oh, Elizabeth, go on. Brother Byrd is our guest. Your homework can wait."

I had to obey Daddy.

By the time we got into the cornfield, I was so scared that I immediately ran away again. The same thing happened a third time. Then he stopped asking me. From that point on, I avoided him every time I saw him. I would not even join the family in listening to him play the saw, which he loved to do to entertain us. I was so confused, so mixed up about what was going on in my body. I think that's when I began to hate being a girl. I didn't know what I was doing to make him do what he was doing, but somehow I felt it was my fault. I was to blame.

Years later, in retirement, he moved into town three houses away on our street. He often came by our house, and my response was always the same. Yuk. Repulsion. Guilt. I always got away from him as fast as I could. And without knowing why, I always felt ashamed of my body.

I was a "Daddy's girl" in those early teen years. I loved being with him. Several intimate memories still give me a warm sense of his wisdom and care. I thought he was God because of the things he did when we were together. One day, I followed him as he used the binder to cut wheat in the big field beside the lane. He roused a nest of baby rabbits and immediately called "Whoa" to the horses, Prince and King, who were pulling the binder. Then he climbed off, and set the babies in a safe place beside a cut area and said to me "I would never want to hurt God's creatures." He held one for me to stroke the soft fur, then put it in the nest with the others, climbed up on the machine and continued mowing the field.

Another day, on a Sunday afternoon walk in the meadow beside the creek, he suddenly said, "Elizabeth, stop and take a look at what is on the ground almost under your feet." I paused, looked, and saw a whole patch of purple violets. "Keep your eyes open, Elizabeth. Never tramp on the beauty of God's amazing creation. Give thanks always that you can see it, and be a part of it." He stooped and picked one, held it up for me to smell it.

An intimate moment that was burned into my memory in those formative years influenced my life for all my years after. I was sitting with Daddy at sunset on the limestone, gray, rugged wagon shed wall facing west. It was one of those Sunday times I treasured, when he took time for me alone, and we talked about important things.

Daddy: "What do you want to be when you grow up, Elizabeth?" Without a pause, I said, "A preacher like you, Daddy."

Silence for a long moment, then, Daddy said: "Well, you're a girl. You could be a missionary, or perhaps a Christian educator."

Women were not allowed to be ordained in those days. Being born a girl meant, once again, lack of privilege. It colored my relationship with every pastor I had. Forty years later, in 1972, things had changed, and I asked Daddy how he would feel about my being ordained, which I wanted to do. I told him what he had said way back on the wagon shed wall forty years before. Tears filled his eyes, and he said, "I can't remember ever saying that. I'm sorry that I kept you from being a minister. I will be very proud and happy if you decide to be ordained now."

I was ordained in 1975, just after I graduated from getting my Doctor of Divinity degree from a consortium of theological schools in Dayton, Ohio. I felt as if a dream had been fulfilled.

I was a sophomore in high school when the English teacher, Emily Miller, discovered I was severely near-sighted. We were studying pronunciation at the time. She had written on the blackboard: "Will you be gone long" and asked us to punctuate it. Being in the back of my row I squinted hard and tried to make sense of what looked like, "Will you be gone, Dong." Finally, assuming "Dong" was a name, I wrote "Will you be gone, Dong?"

Miss Miller called me to her desk. "Elizabeth, are you trying to be funny?"

I was embarrassed, explained that I could not see the board. She called my parents to say I needed to see an eye doctor.

Dr. H. Grant Preston was the only optometrist in town, Daddy's friend. He asked Daddy to stay in the waiting room. My first examination with Dr. Preston aroused in me terrible feelings of shame. He took me into his dark room, explaining that he needed to look for "waxen kernels."

He then fondled my breasts, telling me that I shouldn't tell my father about this procedure. I remembered Mama's reaction to Frank, and knew there was something wrong about this. I begged not to go back to him. I did not tell Daddy why, enduring those annual visits for several years. I kept wondering what I was doing that caused him to act this way. It never occurred to me to blame him. Years later, when I told my sister Margaret about it, she said, "That dirty old man!" He had done the same thing to her! And, doubtless, to dozens of other young girls! God trouble his soul. It makes me mad still, to realize how very vulnerable young girls are to abusive old men! And it is still happening all over the world!

Now I know that millions of young girls in this world are going through abuses too horrible to imagine. In parts of India and Africa, girls as young as seven are being taken from their parents, married off to old men who expect them to labor like slaves and be sex partners on call at any moment. Millions of girls are subjected to clitoridectomies and other abusive surgical practices in order to enhance man's sexual pleasure and dull their own. Trafficking in girls in many parts of the world is a lucrative business; foot-binding in China is illegal but still practiced.

As a child and a growing teen in those very unsettling 30's, I was only vaguely aware that the Great Depression was crushing the life and vitality out of millions in the middle and lower classes of society. I did not know that workers everywhere were confronting the unjust distribution of wealth. Labor unions were springing up in response.

Even the "absolutes" of the Christian faith, which prevailed in my home, were being questioned. I was too young then to know that the most prominent theologian of the century, Paul Tillich, had replaced my beloved dogma, "Our Heavenly Father," with God as "The Ground of Being." This was a radical shift that took the anthropomorphic "God in the sky" and fixed "Him" in the heart of every individual believer.

The sanctity of marriage, defined as sexual exclusivity and lifelong commitment to one person of the opposite gender, began to tremble at the roots; divorce became common. Fixed roles of female and male were quaking in their boots. The woman's sphere as isolated inside the home, caretaker for children and helpmate for husband, no longer satisfied or seemed immutable. Man's self-defined acceptance of male as "the norm" was being contested, then soundly rejected as the Women's Liberation Movement got into full swing. Male privileges outside the home as breadwinner and decision maker began to be questioned and challenged. Technological advances brought ever more startling and unimaginable products and possibilities. Change was the order of the day, radical, at the roots, change. Steadily, as the century moved into its fullness, there was a groundswell of testing every "given."

I knew nothing of economic theory, but as I moved from childhood into the teen years, I was often reminded of the fact that there was no money for the things I wanted, that all our money had to go to the land bank.

I was twelve when I became really embarrassed about my

incorrigibly straight hair. I asked Mama if I could have a set of curlers, which, as I remember, cost a dollar and thirty-nine cents. She said "We will have to ask Daddy."

He said without hesitation, "No, Effie, you know that we don't have any money for frivolous things. Besides, I don't want Elizabeth to think that she has to have curly hair to be beautiful." The answer was "NO." Final.

I was mad at Daddy. But I blamed Mama for needing to ask him in the first place. Why couldn't she make such a decision on her own? In those teen years, my relationship with Mama seemed to be always "on edge." I wanted from her, and never got it, those sweet, intimate times I had with Daddy. I was sure she liked the boys better than she liked me. I was embarrassed by her wearing an old tan coat with faux fur year after year. I decided that when I got to be grown up that I would NOT be like Mama.

Looking back now I realize that there was no money for a new coat for her because she spent it all on shoes for us kids.

I did enjoy all the old adages she used all the time. When I did a sloppy job dusting or sweeping, I was likely to hear:

> *When a task is once begun,*
> *Never leave it 'till it's done.*
> *Be the labor great or small,*
> *Do it well, or not at all.*

Those were the days when Daddy cut our long, yellow pencils in two at the beginning of the school year, and we took turns getting the eraser half. He always said, "You need to make this last through January, so be careful how you sharpen it."

We could not afford to buy tablets for doing our homework. Instead we used torn-open envelopes for scratch paper.

We went barefooted from the first of May to the opening of school. There was no money for shoes during the warm summer months.

When I was nearly twelve, several of my girlfriends began to take piano lessons from our church pianist, Wilda Cline, and I begged Daddy to let me take them, too. He said, "You must wait a little while. Wilda is careless with her time. I want you to have the best teacher we can find." Several months later, he told me to my delight that I would start lessons with Ruth Weybright, the college music professor in Bridgewater. I gobbled it up, never was reminded to practice and in wintertime, my fingers often hurt with cold as the piano was kept in the parlor, a room with no heat.

Many years later, I learned that "because Brother Glick is a trustee of the college and cannot afford to pay," those early years of lessons were free, a gift from Ruth Weybright herself. I was blessed on two counts: Daddy knew music and what was best for me, and Ruth Weybright was the soul of generosity, and gave me a lifetime legacy. I became a music teacher, privileged and thankful. I love playing the piano still, a comfort in my old age.

When my youngest brother, Stanley, my eighth brother, was born on April Fool's Day in 1932, he completed the dozen. My family was the mainstay of my life. I thought of us as "the fours—the four big boys, the middle mixture and the three little kids." We nicknamed all of us: Bendell, (Wendell), Dictor (Victor), Pune (Junior), Bane (Wayne), Libus (Elizabeth),

Duck (Donald), Morgue Horn (Margaret), Josephus Alphonso Gingercake (Joseph), Pep (Dawn), Poop (Ruth) and Salty and Salty (Paul and Stanley).

After supper (only "hifalutin" people said "dinner"), it was homework time. We all gathered around the big, dinner table, and Daddy became the teacher he had become when we had moved to the farm. He was the principal at Centerville Elementary for several years. There was no goofing off, delaying, no talking until everyone had completed their work and left the table. And, before leaving, each one submitted their work to Daddy and received approval. With the perspective of over eighty years, I am so thankful for those early years when there was no such thing as flaunting authority. Also, the expectations of children's cooperation in family tasks were clear and firm. We learned that our contributions to the smooth working of the family were important, essential.

At first I felt lost in the big brick house far out in the country. I longed for home. One day I remember myself standing in the middle of the big dining room, disoriented, crying, needing to ask Wendell which way it was to the kitchen.

Gradually the new house became home to me. Taking piano lessons soothed my homesickness, and I soon began to accompany our hymn sings each Sunday evening as we would all gather around the piano to sing. Hymns were our favorites: "What a Friend We Have in Jesus" and "Trust and Obey." Folk tunes were a close second. "Home on the Range," "Seeing Nellie Home."

Daddy's strong bass and Mama's clear, sweet soprano still resound in memory. Sometimes I long still for those simple, secure and largely unworried days. I was wrapped snugly in myself, as teens tend to be, content to dream my own dreams and imagine my own future. I assumed that after I graduated from North River High School, I would go to college at Bridgewater, five miles from the farm, a bus ride away. Wendell, six years my senior, had already graduated from Bridgewater. It was expected that he would get a job and send money home for my tuition. That was the way it was to be for all twelve of us.

In college I would be a music major, continuing my lessons with my beloved teacher, only, now on organ *and* piano. I would graduate with a Bachelor of Science in Music Education *Magna cum Laude,* and become a public school music teacher. There was no choice in the matter, it seemed, and I accepted it as a happy situation. I would live at home and go and come each day with Vic, Wayne and Johnnie as day students.

I was eager, and only vaguely aware that international affairs in faraway Europe would reach right down into my family's life, and my own, to disrupt this privileged dream.

Mama had said "No dates till you're 16." When I got interested in boys, it seemed to me that my brothers had some weird need to embarrass me in front of my date. The first time it happened, Mama caught on and nipped it in the bud. I was sixteen. It was my first date. Roy had asked me if he could pick me up and take me to the church where the youth group was having a birthday party for one of our members. I was excited, and said "yes."

When the day came, several of the boys were up on the roof atop the front door on the long porch with rope and a bucket of water, when Mama caught them and put a stop to the whole enterprise! They were about to rig up a way to have Roy soaked when he opened the door!

A week before I graduated in 1939, I was stricken with abdominal pain, rushed to the hospital, and had the first of nine surgeries that I was to experience during my long life. Appendicitis. As a typically self-centered teenager, I felt important that I had to be carried up the steps to walk across the stage to receive my diploma.

In the late thirties, the old stand-up radio was the only connection we had beyond the confining boundaries of the nearly 200-acre farm. From that old radio, we learned of the gathering storm across Europe, with Adolph Hitler's conquest of Poland and the ensuing involvement of Britain and France. Japan was at war with China. FDR and Congress were embroiled in arguments between ardent isolationists and those who believed the US should join our Allies by entering the war and stopping Germany's ambition to overtake Europe and annihilate the Jews.

On the home front, people with money were lining up in front of movie houses to see Margaret Mitchell's "Gone With the Wind," a picture of life in the deep South. My peers fed nickels and dimes into roadhouse jukeboxes to hear the latest folk singer. I heard about these things, but had no money to join them. Inside the family and outside in the culture, it was the time of Prohibition and Moonshine. John Barleycorn, The Women's Christian Temperance Union, Teetotalers and avid drinkers. Mama was a committed WCTU member. She had us kids sign the pledge to never drink alcohol. It read, "On my honor, I declare that while I live I will not drink alcoholic beverages. From all tobacco I'll abstain and never take God's name in vain." I signed it. Some of my brothers rebelled.

John Titus (first row center) with his four daughters
(left to right) Ruth, Beth, Margaret, and Dawn—
and seven of his eight sons (second row, left to right)
Victor, Donald, Johnny, Wendell, Joe, Stanley, and Wayne.

Four

THE FEARFUL, FULFILLING, FIGHTING FORTIES

"Returning violence for violence multiplies violence,
adding deeper darkness to a night
already devoid of stars.
Darkness cannot drive out darkness;
Only light can do that.
Hate cannot drive out hate; only love can do that."[5]

Days are the backbone of a lifetime. The playwright,
Herb Gardner said, 'You have to own your days and
name them each one of them, or else the years go right
by and none of them belong to you.' Paradoxically, a
day can be longer than a season. You cannot live an
autumn, but you can live an autumn day."[6]

On the political scene, FDR had challenged tradition by winning a third term as President of the United States. In his State of the Union address in January 1940, he set a different tone than the typical one of isolationism in regard to foreign affairs. He asked Congress to finance the greatest peacetime military buildup in the history of the country. This was greeted by a strong third of the nation, my family included, with consternation and rage. It was seen as "a drift toward war." The winter and spring months of 1941 saw seventy committees and many church pronouncements spring up in opposition to taking sides. Ignoring the opposition, in June, Senator Edward Burke and Representative James Wadsworth brought before Congress the Selective Training and Service Bill which called for the first peacetime draft in the nation's history. Words like "Warmonger" and "Interventionist" sounded in thunderous objection. Families were split apart; relationships were broken over differences of opinion as to whether to go to war or not. A girl cousin of mine said to sister Margaret, "Your brother Johnnie has a yellow streak down his back." It was a common way to describe conscientious objectors and non-combatants as "cowards." Mickie didn't even speak to Phyllis for years afterward.

The draft bill became law on September 16 and the nation began to move steadily into preparations for war. All the systems of manufacturing and industry were asked to change into production of things needed to make weapons. Homes were in upheaval, as wives and mothers, once thought to be guardians of the home front, now left their homes by thousands to join the ranks of "working people." "Rosie the Riveter" became the model of female strength to do jobs originally limited to men only. Speakers in Women' Clubs all over the place challenged women to be "the ones who will break the cycle of war."

The US seemed to be in a race to out-do Germany in production of tanks, bombs and all sorts of materials to support the war effort. Women spent untold hours preparing bandages, scrimping to fit food rationing quotas. Entertainment of GIs became big business for many.

The decade of the 40's saw the advent of bobby socks. "Adolescents" turned into "teenagers" to be catered to by commercial interests, a time to be prolonged and enjoyed. Sloppy, baggy bluejeans, long shirttails, became the norm, and the urge to look like everybody else was the driving force.

On December 7, 1941 Japan bombed Pearl Harbor, severely damaging the US Pacific Fleet. To the public it was presented as a "bolt out of the blue" a sneak attack totally unexpected. I did not know until many years afterward that there had been growing tension between our two governments for decades. As a matter of fact, on the day the attack occurred, the US had sunk a Japanese ship in waters that the US declared to be our own. The very next day, Congress voted to declare war on Japan and the vote was 470 to 1. Jeanette Rankin, objected out of "dictates of her own conscience."

What happened in the wake of that decision is appalling, a shameful blot on American history, a cause for deep remorse and reparation. There were 175,000 people of Japanese descent living in America at the time. Of those, 110,000 lived on the West Coast. 70,000 of those had been born in the US and were bona fide American citizens. Overnight they became a threat to the nation's security, reviled, hated and abhorred, named "Japs," betrayers.

Rage and outright racism were rampant everywhere. The very next day after the Pearl Harbor attack, funds belonging to Japanese Americans were frozen and banks refused to cash their checks. The state of California revoked all licenses to practice law and medicine. All Japanese, citizen or not, were banned from military service. Hateful abuses piled one on top of another. In February 1942, evacuations were encouraged, adding insult to injury. Fifteen Army-run Assembly Centers were quickly designated as receiving centers for internees, who lived in barracks behind barbed wire and were treated as "prisoners of war." Governors protested their coming. They were considered with suspicion and distrust everywhere they went.

In March, the War Relocation Authority was created. Evacuation was no longer invitational; it became compulsory. The internees were moved once again, this time to internment camps located in "dismal places" around the country like deserts and remote areas. Each person was given a number and assigned a place, and all were under the watch of armed army guards night and day.

My church, in shame over the inhumanity being perpetrated against US citizens, assigned people to the various camps to help ease the horrific pain and grief over the misery, humiliations and loss of privacy in the peoples' daily existence.

A special friend of mine, Mary Blocher Smeltzer, spent several years in Manzanar, a camp in desert country to the east of the spectacular Sierras of Northern California. From her I learned the horror of it all, along with the remarkable resilience of the Japanese people in creating new life under such inhumane and unconscionable conditions.

Brother Vic was caught in the draft and made the decision to "stop Hitler." He was among the troops that invaded North Africa in 1942. Weekly letters to Mama and Daddy were a source of eager anticipation. In June 1944, General Dwight D.

Eisenhower was urging his troops to "victory in the invasion of France."

Last summer, as a part of our family's vacation, my son and his family took me to Manzanar, where plans are going forward to build fitting memorials to what happened there. The emotions of shame and sorrow are still raw in me.

Let's face it: America is a nation of aggression and arrogance. First, the takeover of Christopher Columbus and the resultant wars and destruction of the American Indian's life and culture. Then the suspicion, distrust and abuse of all people of Japanese descent. The horrendous blot of black slavery, white claims of superiority, domination and downright hatred and abuse of people because of the color of their skin persists to the present day. We are even today interfering in the internal affairs of the countries of the Arab Spring. Struggles between religions persist. Everywhere there are movements for human rights, women's rights, children's rights, lesbian, gay, transgender rights, power struggles. People everywhere, waking up to their thirst for freedom to live as they choose. Dignity and freedom became the driving force in the society at large.

At the same time, in 1944, in New York City, the arrival of Frank Sinatra, with his silky, tender, alluring voice echoed of Bing Crosby and turned the teenage population into frenzied, swooning, screaming meemies.

If you believe that one person can't make a difference, look at Adolph Hitler. Or, as the Dalai Lama once said, "Go to sleep with a mosquito."

Hitler's ambition and hatred of the Jews, and Roosevelt's will to support our Allies to stop him, reached right down into my family, our conversation around the dining room table, and indeed the very lives of my five brothers who were then eligible for the draft. At that time, girls were not considered suitable for going to war. Ironically, this meant that my life in college and my dreams for the future could go on relatively undisturbed

I was well into my college career as planned in 1940, as the five brothers faced difficult and unsettling decisions.

Deep struggle and sadness permeated my parents' conversations. The central belief of our church was "War is wrong; it is sin." "Live at peace with all 'men.'" "Under no circumstances should guns be used to settle differences."

The opposing sides were set: answer the call of your country and go to war to stop tyranny against a whole race of people, or be true to the God of Peace; declare yourself to be a conscientious objector and work out your stint of the draft with activities like nursing, building bridges, repairing highways or similar assigned tasks. The choices were heart-wrenching for my parents, my brothers, and those of us who loved them all.

For "the boys," the months of 1940 and 41 demanded leaving college, meeting draft boards and disrupting all personal goals. It resulted in these decisions: Wendell would be exempt from military service because of extreme myopia so that he was free to enroll in Virginia Polytechnic Institute. There he would learn plumbing and carpenter skills in order to help my parents to upgrade facilities in the farmhouse.

Brother Vic was caught in the draft and made the decision to "stop Hitler." He was among the troops that invaded North Africa in 1942. Vic's choice to join the army meant that he was sent almost immediately to join combat troops in Africa.

The day he started up the lane to go to his unknown future, the whole family broke into tears and sobbing.

Junior, now Johnnie, was a non-combatant, assigned to be a cook in a returning veterans' camp in the cold mountain regions of Pennsylvania. He later applied for and was trained to be a nurse at Alexian Brothers Hospital in Chicago. That led to his being in medical school and becoming a family doctor later back home in Broadway, Virginia. Wayne was excused because he had been ordained as a minister of the church and was permitted to continue his studies at the college.

Don was a conscientious objector, after having had to face a skeptical, probing draft board to prove he really did have conscientious objection to carrying a gun and possibly killing another man. He was sent to serve in the army hospital in Denver, Colorado. Joe, Paul and Stanley were under age of the draft.

We were torn apart as a family. No more would we all be together, boisterous, growing, secure and happy.

What was happening to us was happening to millions of families and men everywhere. Fear and anxiety took over across the nation. Gas and food rationing produced scarcities and uneasiness. Bacon grease, old automobile tires and any kind of tin were saved in enormous piles for the war effort.

Ironically, because I was born female, I was only remotely affected by the war. Even though boys disappeared from college classes every day, and the only ones left were 4-F or pre-ministerial students, physically unfit for military service, like Wendell, I continued my personal goals steadily.

Three summers during college days, I became a Bible School Teacher in the mountains of Wild West Virginia. I was hired by the District Board of the Church of the Brethren. I lived with parishioners of the various little churches, and I learned a lot about poverty, bed bugs and the generosity of those who have very little of the world's goods.

One summer I served as secretary for the Church of the Brethren District Executive, A. Stauffer Curry. In preparation for that job, I took a quick course in shorthand and became a proficient typist. I enjoyed that summer, and have been glad many times that I have those skills.

My first year after graduation from college, with the dream of becoming a minister still fresh in my mind, I spent pursuing my Master of Divinity Degree at Bethany Theological Seminary in Chicago. It was my introduction to big city life. As we registered, all the incoming girls were required to meet with the Dean of Women. Carrie Summers warned us that it was dangerous in the city for women on the streets, especially at night. She said we should never be without a way to protect ourselves, to carry at all times the 3-inch-long hatpin which she gave each of us. I thought surely that would never happen to me.

About a month later, I was hired as the church organist at the Presbyterian Church in Cicero, about twenty miles west of the city. It required coming home late at night on Thursdays following choir practice, a long walk to the El followed by a 20-minute ride. One such night, I was terrorized when I became aware that a stalker was following me. When I could feel his hot breath on my neck, I reached for the hatpin, sunk it into his thigh, and heard his piercing scream, as I fled to the nearest unlocked vestibule in a row house. I crouched there until I heard him pass in rage. I waited a long time, my heart racing, before I headed again to the El and joined the unaware mass of riders going wherever they were headed. Carrie gave me a second hatpin the next day.

I really enjoyed the two courses I took at Bethany, "The Bible for the Modern World" and "Church History." But my time there was cut short. Daddy and Mama needed more money than I could pay with my organist job.

It so happened that in June 1945, I got a job offer dumped in my lap by our Doctor Miller's daughter, Dorothy. She had held the job of Music Supervisor, of Summit Township, Somerset County, Pennsylvania, and was leaving it to get married. I left the seminary reluctantly, took a trip to Pennsylvania, applied for, and got the job.

That called for major changes in my life. I would travel between seven, mostly rural one-room schools in Meyersdale and vicinity.

The job required driving daily, and I did not own a car—or know how to drive one. On the very day that I was hired by Superintendent Galen Peck, he took me shopping for the shiny blue 1935 Chevy I bought with great excitement. Then he gave me my first driving lesson. I also rented a room that very day in Meyersdale, Pennsylvania, in the home of Besse and Guy Floto.

I yearned for the safe home I had known. Everything was new, strange, demanding. The Flotos' support eased my fears and loneliness. They became surrogate parents. I got a big kick out of Besse's favorite epithet at drivers who got in her way on the streets. "Move it or milk it," she would shout from behind her own wheel. Guy gave me the encouragement I needed to tackle the challenges and changes that were coming at me pell-mell. The Flotos fed me well, and showed interest in my comings and goings. They even arranged with their niece, L. Blubaugh, to take me out on a blind date, which put me in the back seat with a guy whose gonads were doing overtime and whose intentions with girls were a million miles away from mine with guys. I was never again so glad to get away from a man. And much more wary as to what risks I would take with them.

The job was to teach teachers and children the rudiments of music required by the state for eligibility to enter high school. Looking back, I see how determined I was to do my job well. I made lesson plans, taught them to the teachers who then were to teach them to the children. I often felt the teachers resented me, that I interfered with the time they needed to teach "the basics of reading, writing and arithmetic." Besides, my salary was a third higher than theirs. And I was a demanding newbie!

In the summer before my second year of teaching August 14, 1945, V-J Day announced that the war with Japan was over. I was sad not to be at home to greet my brothers. They immediately continued their education using the generous GI Bill.

My year with the Flotos provided for me the family that I missed and longed for. It also provided the place where I would meet the man of my dreams, and experience that erotic and exotic bloom of "new love" and romance, unlike any time before or since.

I moved at the end of August 1945 into the home of the pastors, Loren and Claire Bowman, and became organist in the Church of the Brethren in Meyersdale.

The letter came on October 20, 1946, and I quickly realized that the other two guys that I thought I wanted to marry were really passing fancies. I am ashamed to admit that I was engaged to marry both CB and CW, one year after the other.

The letter changed my life forever. It was from "848 Sheridan Ave., Pittsburgh 19, Penna, October 10, 1946." It read:

Dear Miss Glick,

By this time you are probably wondering just who I am and why the letter. First of all, allow me to introduce myself. I believe that you know my brother (Wayne) who is the pastor of the Waynesboro, Virginia, Church of the Brethren congregation. I understand that your home is also somewhere in that area.

I am not at all certain that this letter will even reach you. I do know that you were the music supervisor either in Meyersdale or in the adjoining township during the past school year. Perhaps you are no longer there since teaching positions are rather plentiful or you may have wanted to teach nearer home.

To get to the point of this letter, I am wondering whether you would be willing to go to a football game, or to a symphony concert or some other musical event, or simply to a movie sometime with me—sight unseen. There is always something going on in Pittsburgh over weekends and teachers' lives do become lonely at times. I was a mathematics teacher before spending four years in the Army. And am now doing full-time graduate work in Psychology at the University of Pittsburgh.

My home is in Somerset and I manage to drive over there practically every weekend. So if you will let me know concerning your reactions to these suggestions perhaps we can arrange something to do either in Pittsburgh or Somerset one of these days. Perhaps you know my other brother, Dwight, also—He mentioned that he had seen you somewhere.

I hope you will not consider me too presumptuous in writing to you in this manner.

Sincerely,
Glenn W. Rieman

I was not about to spend the night in Pittsburgh with a strange man. We settled on a Sunday afternoon hike in Somerset on a hilly horse farm whose owner he knew.

When Glenn Walker Rieman strode into my life on October 20, everything was different. My heart skipped a beat when his white Oldsmobile parked on Main Street in Meyersdale and his brown jodhpurs brought him up to the Floto's doorstep. We did not miss a weekend together after that day.

In February, after playing around verbally with getting married, we arranged to take a trip to Virginia, to satisfy Glenn's need to follow the tradition of getting the father's permission. All my brothers would be home that weekend. Little did I know what they had in mind! True to form, they accomplished their intention when we arrived.

My parents owned an elegant black leather chair, used only when there was company, constructed to become a recliner. When a certain pin was removed, it lunged backward whenever anyone sat in it suddenly. Without warning, it would throw the person head over heels.

Unbeknownst to Mama, that day the boys had rigged the chair by taking out the pin. The inevitable happened. Mama was mortified. I was mad at my brothers and very embarrassed. Glenn was a good sport, picked himself up and laughed it off.

When it came time for us to leave, I realized that Glenn had not asked Daddy for "my hand." It was the first time that I had ever been really annoyed with him. He had not asked me, either, and in those days, I expected that. As we left to go back to Pennsylvania, I felt tension between us, and wondered what would happen next.

We were about a mile from the farm, on the road past Centerville. Not a word between us. The gorgeous backdrop of the blue Alleghenies stretched down the Valley to the West, when Glenn said, "Beth, will you marry me?" I was so annoyed that he had not asked Daddy, that I made him wait for two miles later. As the road forked into Bridgewater. I simply said, "Yes," and snuggled close to him. Years later, I told him of my frustration.

Even now, I think of that ritual as an indication of inequality in the marriage. Though I was stuck in it as he was, for us it was a silly waste of time and energy. We both knew the answers before the questions were asked. And his regard for me as his equal had already been set, although we didn't always live it out.

Seven and a half short months later, on June 7, 1947 we were married in the little white, frame Summit Church of the Brethren in the heart of the Valley. (The story of our wedding is told in full in my book, *Peace Train to Beijing and Beyond.*)

My wedding day was a day of sublime happiness except for

one thing. With the perspective of years, it seems like a really little thing. At the time, it distressed me greatly. I came into the church for the rehearsal the night before to discover that Stanley, my youngest brother and a singer in the ceremony, was as bald as a bat. He had shaved his head! I didn't know his motivation, but it felt to me like a mean trick. One more brother playing a joke on his sister.

It gives me the shivers now to realize that in the ceremony I had my father "give me away." I now know that that act, alongside the tradition of having the groom accompanied by the officiating minister, symbolizes the ancient tradition of male ownership of the female, first, by the father, then by the husband. I now believe this tradition symbolizes domination of male over female and leads to many of the ills in marriages in our present society; i.e. wife battering and all kinds of abuse in the home.

I regret that it was in my ceremony, but it was.

When I am asked to be the minister now, I will no longer officiate when the couple insists on including that "giving away" stuff. Or, I insist that the father is accompanied by the mother in that part of the ceremony.

In our ceremony, I was thrilled to have Daddy's arm as I walked toward that black-suited wall of males waiting for me in the front of the church. As we joined them, Daddy stepped over beside Loren Bowman, and they together led us through the ceremony that Glenn and I had created.

Our vows were the centerpiece: " I will love, honor and cherish you always." Simple and profound. Lasting beyond death, always. How well I know.

With the perspective of all these years, I know how true it is that love is not ended by the death of a spouse. Love lives on in my memory that blesses and comforts the days when the loved one is no longer present in human form.

I was "in seventh heaven" on that honeymoon night when we left behind the people and the busy-ness of preparing all the trappings of the wedding and sped away down the honey-suckle-scented Valley to Ingleside Hotel in Staunton. Basking in that unrepeatable bliss of new love, we gave ourselves completely to one another. It was our Camelot.

We did not know then that, like JFK's, our "shining moment" would be short-lived and agonizing, as we would need to go through five years of waiting for that first pregnancy to fulfill our dream of parenthood.

Five

THE SHAMEFUL, FLOWING FIFTIES

"The road goes ever on and on,
Down from the door where it began.
Now far ahead the Road has gone,
And I must follow, if I can,
Pursuing it with eager feet,
Until it joins some larger way
Where many paths and errands meet.
And whither then? I cannot say.[7]

Whatever you can do or dream, you can begin it.
Boldness has genius, power, and magic in it.[8]

As I entered the fifties, I was still yearning for a child. The medical profession took us through all sorts of machinations in an effort to help us. In that process, they said after testing the strength of Glenn's sperm, that they were thinking of "using him as a stud." It takes away a bit of the romance of making love when it is foreordained and the place is the doctor's office. And, as the self-blamer I am, I was sure I was the deficient one.

After years of being disappointed every month, we decided to adopt a child. Two more years with visits and analysis of our "ability to care for a child" brought us to the day when I missed a period. Two days later, the social worker told us there was a baby boy available for adoption! She sensed our reticence immediately, and asked why. She was guardedly happy for us. "We will wait and see," she said. "Let me know as soon as you know."

It was indeed the miracle we had been waiting for. Peggy was on the way! She was born on United Nations Day, October 24, 1952. It began a decade of my giving birth every two years, with the inevitable sleep deprivation and dirty diapers. Four girl babies: Jill Christine on January 22, 1955, Marta Elizabeth on January 24, 1947, and Linnea, January 4, 1959, born dead.

The first three were by natural childbirth, so that I could be there in that astonishing moment when a live baby emerged from my womb. That is a singular, unrepeatable moment, that moment when a hearty cry signals the arrival of an infant who has lived inside one's own body, who is now mine to love, care for, and watch as she grows to full womanhood.

For me, that astonishment was new with each baby, except the dead one.

I had known that the full term fetus had died ten days before, so, following the doctor's advice, as I so often did in those days, I chose not to be awake to hear the awful silence of death at the instant of her birth. It was a choice I will always regret. Birthing Linnea on January 4, 1959, opened for me a great unknown sorrow. I weep still that doctors thought it wise that I not even see her. Once again I thought that males knew better than I. I am sad still that I put their word over what my heart wanted.

Almost four years later, on September 25, 1962, as the nurse called out "It's a boy!," I felt that unbelievable wonder as I gathered Eric in my arms the instant after he was born. Astonishing! New life! A son! A full family circle!

While I was birthing all these white babies, fulfilling my dream of motherhood, in the sizzling South a black seamstress named Rosa Parks grew tired of giving in to an unjust Jim Crow law that required that she give up her seat on a bus to a white passenger who claimed it. It was December 1, 1955; Jill was less than a year old. Rosa defied the law and gained her rightful freedom as an American citizen. Soon thereafter, rage over the injustice, indignity and demeaning of one person and a whole race more, led to an outright explosion called the Civil Rights Movement that quickly came to full boil and struggle. I would teach those babies of mine to honor Rosa Parks as I had been taught to respect Mr. Pleasant, our black neighbor, long years before.

I loved being a mother, watching my beloved children grow and choose their personal wishes and desires. It was hectic and demanding, too. Music played a central part in our lives during those busy days. I taught piano lessons in order to have a bit of "spending money." I added all the children to my list of students.

Even though they all played piano, each one had a special instrument that they thought of as their own. Peggy chose to be a violinist and was chosen as the Youth Guest for a performance with the Dayton Philharmonic when she was a Junior in high school. Jill chose cello. She was a creative, happy child, given to unexpected thinking, a risk-taker, climbing towers and walking ledges on mountaintops. In restaurants, to her father's embarrassment, she made friends with everyone there. She was delightfully open and easy with strangers, except for her first grade teacher who had a special liking for boys and long, red fingernails that scared her.

One day Jill came home for lunch, walked over to me and beat me with her fists. When I asked her what was wrong, she screamed, "I hate Mrs. Z!"

Glenn and I went to the principal and asked to transfer her out of that school, but the answer in those days was, "No." Parents had no choice in the matter. Jill developed nightmares and cried out in her sleep. I still feel sad that she had to endure the agonies of that long nine months. I wish I had defied the rules and saved her. In spite of the difficulties with that first grade teacher, Jill was an exuberant child, free-spirited, always thinking and feeling "outside the lines." After choosing cello as her special instrument, she loved it from the start, and, to this day, she plays the classics, along with her own improvisations, with soul and ease. The baby-grand piano occupies a central place in her living room and life, but the cello is her soul love.

Marta, with the curly black hair, was steady and solemn, always wanting to please. Like her sisters before her, she was a serious student, dependable, responsible, respectful of authority. The one exception to that was at age 14, when she scared us by disappearing into her room every day after school and spending the hours 'til supper there. We wondered and worried about what might be happening at school. Then, Christmas came and our fears were allayed when she presented us with a beautiful blue/green full size afghan she had crocheted herself. Marta was always a self-starter, carving out her life from any possibilities at hand. She wanted to learn to play the flute, and I wanted to get her one. But Glenn nixed it. When I went to him to get him to let me buy one, he said, "Beth, we already have so many instruments. Tell her to play the violin." After a mild argument, I gave in. He was my husband and had the right to choose. A backward glance today from adulthood reveals how completely I bought that "second class" designation of how "a wife gives in to her husband." My deepest regrets are linked to those deprivations of my children.

I gave myself completely to trying to be the best mother in the world. Not knowing at that time that I had bought, hook, line, and sinker, patriarchy's definitions of female fulfillment as being "submissive wife and selfless mother." I was happy in those years. I wanted to be a writer, but I would wait until the children were grown and gone to achieve that dream. The infancy and childhood of my babies was a time of great joy to me.

At the same time, I was aware that a 15 year-old, also an Elizabeth, born black in Little Rock, Arkansas, Elizabeth Eckford, was pursuing her dream of being a lawyer. She knew that the United States Supreme Court, in the famous Brown vs. Board of Education case in 1953, had ruled "separate but equal" unconstitutional. She knew that Central High School, a bastion of white supremacy in her city of 100,000, had been chosen for desegregation in compliance with the Supreme Court ruling. "The Little Rock Nine" had been created for the task. She joined them.

In the midst of that turmoil, on the home front, the call came on July 9, 1955, that my brother, Paul, at age 24, had been killed in a car crash as he was coming home late at night from leading a youth camp in North Carolina. Paul was my "kid brother" and a pre-ministerial student. When sister-in-law Mary called to say "Paul was killed in an automobile accident last night," my first response was "Paul who?"

"Your brother, Paul, Beth." I was stunned. Impossible. No, it can't be! I remember the shock I felt as he lay in his coffin in the parlor and I realized that his spirit was gone, that the brother I knew and loved just was not there, and never would be again. It all seemed so unreal, mysterious. We were no longer twelve kids, but eleven.

It was the fall of 1957, the year of Marta's birth. My dear friend, Lally, mother of five, had said jokingly to me, when she visited me in the hospital the day Marta had first screamed her entrance into the world, "Now, Beth, you're tied to the tree. My mother always said: 'With one you can take it and run. With two, you can do. But with three, you're tied to the tree'."

It was indeed a chaotic time of my motherhood, and of the society at large, but I was so very happy. I hardly had time to enjoy the children's antics and growing. I found their assertions of developing personhood exasperatingly disruptive of my own time, but I also found great joy in the whole process of being a family.

Owning a television set was becoming common. All our friends had them. In order to keep Peggy home from the Schultz neighbors every day, we got our first set in 1953. It brought into our living room the horrors and agonies of black people caught in the raw hatred of southern racism. I watched in absolute horror and shame (and some sense of hurrah) on September 4, 1957, as Elizabeth Eckford, resolute, notebook in hand, joined the flow of students into Central High in Little Rock, Arkansas, as raging white racist Hazel Bryan yelled raw, ugly, racial epithets at her from behind.

When I think now of those awful atrocities of water hoses and mad dogs on the streets of Mississippi and Alabama, the unrest all over the southland that I love, I feel shame for my white race, and want to find ways to heal the breaches between us, wherever they still remain.

Beth's brother Paul

Six

THE SEARING, SEETHING, SIZZLING SIXTIES

There are only two ways to live your life. One is as though nothing is a miracle. The other is as though everything is a miracle.[9]

"You shall know the truth and the truth will set you free."[10]

Family Photo, November 14, 1962.
Peggy, Beth, Jill, baby Eric, Glenn, and Marta.

As the decade of the sixties dawned, (I was in my forties) I thought I was surely the happiest woman in the world. I had a home of my own to keep. I had a husband whose love and job were sure and steady. Having just lost that fourth little daughter at full term birth, I was comforted in my grief in having three others to love and raise as my own. Peggy was six; Jill, four; Marta, two; a trio of joy for me.

There was also Glenn's unfulfilled dream of "having a boy to carry on my name." In those days, there was no such thing as a girl "carrying on her father's name." I felt the sting of that, that having a baby boy was somehow considered "better" than having girls. Thankfully, when each one of the girls was born, Glenn never expressed a word of regret.

As we moved into the sixties, the kids now full of activities and demands, I began to become aware of a certain malaise that was developing in me. In response to it, I felt troubled, and guilty, as if something were "wrong with me." While I was almost oblivious to The Women's Liberation Movement which was gaining strength, I was aware that the sexist language of worship was "getting on my nerves."

I spoke about it with my sister-in-law, Barbara, and she said, "Beth, you are not alone in feeling that way. There are lots of us who feel dissatisfied with the way men assume that we will give up our careers in order for them to do whatever they choose to do. I gave up nursing to move with Wayne to Chicago."

She gave me *The Feminine Mystique* a book by Simone de Beauvoir, a book that connected me to what was happening in the culture as women woke up to their second class citizenship, as defined by males.

That book was a breath of fresh air. I was not alone in my malaise, and it wasn't my fault that even though I had everything I wanted, (a husband, a home, children), I was still asking the question "Is this all there is? Something is missing." When I spoke of this to Barbara, she said, "What's missing is you, Beth. You have given yourself away; you have no life of your own."

I began to read avidly: Mary Daly and John Bianchi's *Beyond God the Father;* Daly's *Gyn/Ecology* and *Pure Lust; Sisterhood is Global,* edited by Robin Morgan; Merlin Stone's *When God Was A Woman;* Rosemary Radford Reuther, *Woman Church; A Different Heaven and Earth* by Sheila Collins; *Making The Connections* by Beverly Wildung Harrison. I just could not get enough. My mind was spinning. My theology was shaking at the foundations.

When each of the girls was born, Glenn never said a word of disappointment. He had greeted each one with "Another girl! Isn't she beautiful? And she has all ten fingers and toes, and everything she needs. And she's healthy!"

But there were our best friends Dick and Lally, pregnant and surprised with their fifth. I'm sure, in retrospect, that Glenn's ego suffered, that their unwanted fifth reinforced in his mind a sense of inadequacy.

We talked about having another baby. "But it's only a 50/50 chance it will be a boy," I said.

"Girls are nice, too," Glenn responded.

So it was that at age 39, right in the midst of my awakening to the Women's Liberation Movement, on September 25, 1962, I gave a very fast birth in Altoona Hospital, Altoona, Pennsylvania, to a 9-pound 2-ounce male child. Glenn was not allowed to be in the room with me. The baby was a "blue baby" with the cord pulled tightly around his neck. The opening moments of his life were ominous, silent, filled with concern and anxiety. Nurses scurrying about. I knew something was wrong. Then, an alert doctor quickly cut the cord, and a lusty howl quieted my fears.

A couple days later, Glenn and I finally came to an agreement about what his name would be.

"Let's call him 'Eric', Glenn said. "And you like 'Douglas', how about 'Eric Douglas'"?

That boy/girl thing flashed through my mind. "I want him to have my name, too. How about 'Eric Glick Rieman'?"

"It's a little hard to say with all those 'icks' in it. But if you want it, that's what it will be." And that's what it was, and still is. I still like the ring of it, "Eric Glick Rieman." He's my son.

In those early years of the 1960's, I felt truly fulfilled. I was full-time mother and housewife. Every day was filled with the non-stop efforts it takes to raise children. Nursing. Diapers. Chores and housework. School activities, PTA. Driving children hither and yon. For all of us, piano lessons, practice schedules strictly adhered to, Recitals. For me, piano teacher on the side, earning the only money I ever saw or controlled during my marriage. Violin lessons with Dr. Katz for Peggy and Marta; Cello with Mr. Bowen for Jill. Brownies and Girl Scouts. Always church on Sundays, Sunday school in the morning, Youth Group in the evening. Extra-curricular activities like spending time at the Living Arts Center once a week, Junior Philharmonic Orchestra rehearsals with Conductor Holeshevsky on Saturday mornings. Trips to the library with time to spend as each one chose a pile of books to occupy leisure time during the coming week. Travel to exotic places during the summers.

We greeted having a new baby in the family with excitement and a sense of adventure. As I nursed Eric and watched him grow, I often felt surprised by the joy that he brought me. One day I grabbed a piece of scrap paper and wrote a poem that I called, "Surprised By Joy."

I was so happy with the three little mothers giving attention and care to their baby brother. It was a time of deep satisfaction and peace for me. But…

SURPRISED BY JOY

I was rudely interrupted today,
I was dully watching TV
when
my small son
climbed on my lap,
blocked my vision
and hugged me so hard
I said, "Ouch!"
He gave me a tickly
wet kiss on my neck
And
quick as a flash
ran away to play

Alongside my nearly complete absorption in my role as mother, there was Glenn, my good husband, who had his own expectations of a wife, including keeping an immaculate house.

One day, he came in from a busy day at work, and wrote on a dusty mantelpiece, "DUST ME!" It had been a hectic day with the four kids. I was hurt, told him I didn't think that was funny. Maybe he could help a bit! I don't remember any other time that I "chafed at the bit." Mostly we both accepted our roles as given by the culture of the day. Roles clear and un-negotiable. Husband as breadwinner, yard worker, caretaker of car maintenance, in charge of finances, taking out the garbage. Wife as child caregiver, cook, dishwasher, housekeeper, launderer, mate, volunteer without pay.

Rarely did either one of us challenge those roles in the early sixties. Our lives were full, demanding, chaotic and bouncing with vitality. Growing children were busy meeting our expectations, finding their own way, developing their own identity. As parents we were secure in our love for each other, engaged with the children in helping them become good citizens, good people, ready to make a contribution to the betterment of the world. We were committed to their full development and happiness. It took all my time, which I gave gladly. We were not fully aware of this at the time but we were mirroring what was going on in the nation at large.

In July 1960, at the Democratic Convention in July, John F. Kennedy, campaigning for the presidency at age 43, said: "What I offer is not a set of promises; it is a set of challenges." Much like the challenges we were experiencing at the home level, he told the nation

"We stand today on the edge of a new frontier—the frontier of the 1960's. A frontier of unknown opportunities and perils, A frontier of unfulfilled hopes and threats. Ask not what your country can do for you, ask what you can do for your country."

At his inaugural address on January 21, 1961, he declared:

Let the word go forth from this time and place...

That the torch has been passed to a new generation of Americans.... So let us begin anew...let us explore the stars, conquer the deserts, eradicate disease...tap the ocean depths, and encourage the arts and commerce....

All this will not be finished in the first one hundred days...the energy, the faith, the devotion we bring to this endeavor will light our country and all who serve it, and the glow from that fire can truly light the world....

There was a sense of excitement and adventure in the air. More than 18,000 people applied to be in the Peace Corps that was created that year. Commitment to causes of all kinds to better the lives of all people were everywhere. Change was the prevailing attitude. For one thousand sparkling days, The White House brimmed over with renovations, style, and the magic of musicians like Pablo Casals, Isaac Stern, and Igor Stravinsky. Pulitzer prizewinner poet Robert Frost read his poetry at the Inauguration. 49 Nobel Prizewinners ate dinner with the President as their host. A current hit show written by Alan Jay Lerner, likened the times to the mythical Court of King Arthur and his Knights of the Round Table. Camelot contained the President's favorite lines, which became eerily appropriate to describe his own "shining moment" as President of the United States:

Don't let it be forgot
That once there was a spot
For one brief shining moment
That was known as Camelot.

"For one brief shining moment," oh, so brief, for one thousand days, it seemed as if everything were possible. JFK's vision for America was, as he said in a speech at Amherst College, "an America which will not be afraid of grace and beauty." Under his presidency, it would be a principled, peace-loving nation, a place where "violence is not strength, and compassion is not weakness." For "one brief moment," strikingly beautiful wife Jackie charmed dignitaries and common people alike. First Lady Jacqueline Bouvier Kennedy was the embodiment of the vision. Young and old were drawn to the couple and the vision as cat to catnip. Causes and slogans popped up everywhere. Hopes were high. And then—I remember the exact moment— as I was contentedly nursing my beloved baby boy while watching the President's motorcade arrive in Dallas. Rifle shots rang out from the gun of 24-year-old assassin Lee Harvey Oswald, who himself was assassinated a day later by the gun of Jack Ruby. In an instant, the vision was cast down, crushed out. The "brief, shining moment" was gone forever.

It was November 1963. I cried out "Oh, No!" Startled, Eric cried with me, and I clutched him closer as if to shield him from a newly dangerous world. I was stunned, in shock. So was my nation. The "perils" of which candidate Kennedy had eloquently spoken had literally taken his life and, for the moment, the hopes and dreams of a whole nation. With all America, I mourned the loss of the dream and the man to make it come true.

But the trajectory was set for change. Unrest was stirring in blacks and women as the Civil Rights and Feminist Movements took hold. Angry Afro-Americans protested and sang,

"We Shall Overcome." Two distinct strands of black resistance sprang up: Martin Luther King with his non-violent, peaceful protest, and Malcolm X and black rage.

Angry women, I among them, thousands of us, marched and sang, "I'm On My Way, and I Won't Turn Back." In the United Nations Conferences in Kenya, Africa, and in Beijing, China we thousands shouted our protests over the inequities between men and women, worldwide.

In the year 2000, at home in Washington, D.C., I had milled with the estimated crowd of 70,000 or so women who filled the mall demanding passage of the Equal Rights Amendment, which has not been passed as law to this day.

In North Carolina and the deep south in the 1960's, however, the patterns of racial segregation were deeply woven into the social fabric." Negroes simply did not sit down with white folks. Yet that's just what happened. Four college youths in North Carolina, who happened to be black, defied the expected norm and were refused service at a lunch counter. They "sat in" in defiance, and started a movement. Sit-ins spread like wildfire to campuses and cities anywhere blacks were refused service. The protest gained strength: there were "read-ins" in all white libraries; "sleep-ins" in the lobbies of segregated motels; "wade-ins" on all-white beaches.

At the same time, in the jungles of a little known country called Vietnam, the US Special Forces, the Green Berets, of the military, were battling what was perceived as a Communist Threat. It was the McCarthy era of suspicion and mistrust.

The House Committee on Un-American Activities decided to investigate Communism in California, They subpoenaed to hearings some local schoolteachers who were involved in leftist causes. They then refused access to students at those hearings. Perceived by the students as a threat to political freedom, a street protest resulted in a policeman being knocked down and beaten. Fire hoses and billy clubs came into play. The riot that ensued lasted an hour and resulted in twelve people injured and 52 carted off to jail. That event galvanized campuses everywhere with a sense of rage and commitment to changing the future by changing the present.

Within minutes of the doctor's announcement of the President's death, in the cabin of the Presidential jet plane at Love Field in Dallas, Vice President Lyndon Johnson took the oath of office to become our 36th President. I was struck by the fact that the transfer of governmental power in our democracy was so easy and smooth.

At for the nation, it was as if a major environmental disaster had hit. Camelot was over, a dream of the past. Bells began to ring; people poured into churches for prayer; work places were stunned into silence, incredibility, shock. Overnight the "New Frontier" with all its promise and youthful vitality and enthusiasm, was replaced by "The Great Society" and the fatherly demeanor of a hulking Texan. He gave the nation a "fleeting sense of security," even as disillusionment set in with the grief and shock.

The restive rumblings between the blacks and whites in the south were reaching fever pitch. A new awareness in the minds of the subjugated and demeaned "Negro" erupted in demands for change and respect. The "slave mentality" which had held firm for years was being contested. Demands for liberty from old, punishing relationships between the races were being acted out to the point of violence and disobedience to expected "norms."

Rosa Parks, a small black woman with large determination, refused to take a back seat on a bus, an action that enabled others to act boldly and courageously for their rights. TV's stark portrayal of the horror of fire hoses and police dogs, chaos and mayhem, people scrambling frantically to escape on the streets of southern cities, are still vivid in my mind. They create a terrible sense of shame and guilt in me for the arrogant behavior of my white race.

A young, dynamic black preacher in Alabama emerged as the leader in a growing movement for full human rights for blacks. Tragedy was mixed with triumph. Martin Luther King Jr. insisted on non-violence and peaceful protest as the way to go. Eldridge Cleaver and Malcolm X, on the other hand touted "Black Power" and violent disobedience. Rage at the absolute injustice of slavery and a culture where my arrogant white race assumed superiority over Afro-Americans was at the boiling point.

Inside my safe home, full of the chaos of raising four children, I began to hear myself asking once again, "Is this all there is? I'm thrilled with these babies and I love Glenn dearly. What's wrong with this picture?" Barbara's comment rang in my ears. "You are what's missing, Beth. You are what's missing!" I knew it was time for me to become active in The Feminist Liberation Movement.

The Civil Rights Movement and the Women's Liberation Movement were one and the same for me—in the struggle for equality and human dignity. I increased my participation in protests and marches. I felt the heady excitement of freedom to work for causes bigger than my own.

I was invited by my church to a weeklong event in personal growth, called "Mission Twelve," and I accepted. For the first time, I was away from the care of the children. I had moments of feeling guilty and selfish. But I came away changed, much more aware of my own needs and wants, my pretenses and excuses.

While the South was boiling over with the rage of "being had," I became a very mad feminist. I was called "bra burner," "man hater," Women's Libber." The day I gave up "Dear Heavenly Father" I felt as if I had truly gone over the brink. My friends accused me of "heresy." Glenn seemed concerned about my emotional stability.

Then, one day as I was wading in the surf, a Bible verse came into my consciousness: "You shall know the truth and the truth will set you free."[11] It is really true, I thought: Father cannot create without Mother. The Women's Liberation Movement is all about claiming the Feminine Divine as fully authentic as "The Heavenly Father." I felt a great freedom and my view of Mama as secondary to Daddy evaporated into thin air. I felt "whole" in a fresh, new way. I literally felt the freedom that comes with truth that transplants the half-truths that limit women or define us as less than male. I also was angry that I had bought "the lie" of the church fathers all those years, I had "been had" and I wouldn't put up with it any longer. Colleagues called me "abrasive." They fought against changing theological language so that it was inclusive. They said I was unreasonable, woman-centered, insisting on my own way, asking them to give up what was sacred to them. The struggles were deep and hard. I felt like a fish out of water, gasping for breath.

For a couple years I stopped going to church entirely and spent Sunday mornings at the ocean, struggling with an emptiness that seemed to engulf my whole existence. Wondering where and when this wilderness would end. Though people that were close to me seemed worried about me, I knew I was right on my journey. I never once wavered toward going back to the way I had thought and talked. I thought of myself as "A holy termite," eating away at the sexist structures that held the women I was working with from taking leadership, deferring to husbands who assumed authority over them.

As the 60's progressed the Civil Rights Movement reached its full potential. I joined the remarkable "March on Washington," where Martin Luther King, Jr. preached his powerful, unforgettable "I Have A Dream" sermon. In 1965, the Civil Rights Act became the law of the land, a major milestone in achieving The American Dream of "liberty and justice for all." A yeasty sense of positive change permeated every organization of the culture. Life as usual would no longer do.

Seven

THE SORROWING, SELF-EMPOWERING SEVENTIES

Beth's daughter Peggy

Cowardice asks the question—is it safe?
Expediency asks the question—is it politic?
Vanity asks the question—is it popular?
But conscience asks the question—is it right?
And there comes a time when one must take a position
That is neither safe, nor politic, nor popular
But one must take it because it is right.[12]

Blessed are they that mourn
for they shall be comforted.[13]

In that national mood, the sorrowing, self-empowering seventies were upon us all. It was the decade of the Encounter Movement, and workshops aimed at personal growth and group development were everywhere.

For me personally, the whole decade of the seventies led from one shocking event to another; Peggy's death on May 20, 1972, topped them all. As self-therapy, in response to that life changing event, I had written and published the book, *Peggy, I May Not Have the Summer.* It paints a picture of that heartrending experience of being a bereaved mother. I enclose Chapter 1 in Appendix A. My identity changed during that decade. I was no longer primarily loved wife and mother. I became primarily Applied Social Scientist, Recognized Professional.

In 1973, I was ordained as a minister in The Church of the Brethren after a 43-year hiatus. On June 5, 1974, I graduated with a Doctor of Ministry Degree from United Theological Seminary and a Consortium of Schools in Dayton, Ohio. From 1975 to 1978 I held the position of "Person Awareness Coordinator" on the national staff of The Church of the Brethren in Elgin,

Illinois. When I was fired from that position in 1978, and was refused a position with The Presbyterian Church, USA, because I was "over-qualified," I created my own business firm. I called it "Human Empowerment in Religion and Society" (HEIRS). I was determined to claim the right of women to be full participants in the leadership of churches and society everywhere.

One weekend we were visiting my sister Dawn and her husband Ray. He had attended one of those workshops. He saw my suffering from a crisis in faith and suggested that I attend an event called "Experiential Theology" led by three skilled social scientists, Ken Mitchell, Bryce Kramer and Bruce Rahtjen.

I spent a whole week away from home and family that September, the first time I was ever apart from them that long. Paying for such an event just for me was a big step in those days. Glenn encouraged me to go, and I stepped through a door that thrust me into a world wider than I ever could have imagined.

Over and over that week I was confronted with Ken's skill in making comments that led me to self-awareness and insights into my own grieving process.

It was during that week that I began to affirm God as a life force that sustains those who suffer, rather than "Heavenly Father" that I had believed as a child. Giving up that concept was truly a "break in my Cosmic egg."

I came home from that workshop with the nascent idea that I wanted to learn how to lead people to new self-awareness as I had been led there. When I mentioned this to Ken, he suggested that I join The Association for Creative Change, (ACC), and take their training courses to become a professional trainer.

ACC was an organization committed to training in four tracks: Personal Development, Group Development, Organizational Development and Conflict Management. Ken was a leader in that group. In 1973, still heavy with grief over the loss of my Peggy, I became a member of ACC and began work in the track called Personal Development. ACC required choosing a mentor to guide me in what I needed to learn and attending further workshops to meet a set of standards and learning goals. I chose Ken as my mentor and spent many hours learning from him the skills he felt I needed. When he thought I was ready, I applied to ACC leaders who evaluated my skills and declared me to be a "Recognized Professional."

In the years that followed, I became recognized in all four tracks and Ken and I became a team. Together, we created a training program called "Caring Ministry" and led these workshops in many churches across the United States and Canada. We were known, by many churches experiencing conflict and seeking skills for handling it, as an effective team.

At the same time, I became more and more aware that I wanted to find some way to join in changing the injustices and abuse against women and girls. I wanted to become active in the Civil Rights Movement for racial justice and freedom. These movements were expanding daily, and I decided that I would devote my life to these causes.

One day in the spring of 1975 I received a call from my church friend, Mary Blocher Smeltzer. For several years, she had been actively urging the General *"Brotherhood"* Board of the Church of the Brethren at the national level to establish a position that would focus on getting women into positions of leadership. Finally it was happening under the rubric, "Person Awareness Coordinator." She asked me to apply for it.

It was the job I had been looking for, except for the name.

Why is it not called "The Role and Status of Women in the Church?" I asked Ralph, the interviewer.

"The church is not ready for that," he said. "The Board (all men) would never fund a position with that name."

"But that's what the position is all about, isn't it?," I insisted.

"That has already been decided," he said. "Will you take the job?" Subject closed. I took the job and set up an office on the college campus near my home in Bridgewater, Virginia.

In September, 1975 I took my first of many trips to attend the Board meeting at the church headquarters in Elgin, Illinois. At that meeting, I was introduced as a new staff member filling the position of "Person Awareness Coordinator." I was greeted warmly at first. Then one of the male executive members of the staff told a joke, a "Dumb Blond" joke. Everybody laughed heartily, everybody but me. When the laughter subsided, I said calmly, "I don't think that joke is funny. It puts women down."

The atmosphere changed. A kind of embarrassment took over the room. People began to leave. It was as if I had said something "not nice," and certainly unnecessary. I felt the boundary I had set for myself. I was on the other side of the full acceptance bar I had felt minutes before. What I had done was to define myself as "the other," and I would live with that reality for all my years on the staff.

"So this is what I'm here for," I said to myself, "to confront sexism everywhere I find it. It won't be an easy road but it's the right thing to do."

I held that job from 1975 to 1978, and it was in fact a challenging and satisfying period of my life.

In 1976 I was awarded my Doctor of Divinity degree. In 1977 I was ordained in the Church of the Brethren. I created and led workshops called "Theological Happenings" for women all over the nation, in the belief that what we believe about ourselves, others and God will determine whether or not we are willing to give gifts of leadership when we are invited to do so.

What I learned about the hidden home life between women and their good, upstanding husbands rocked me at the foundations. Sexism was entrenched, alive and well, in the church and all across this nation. Women were far from free to be their full selves!

I began to preach a sermon I called "Women, Through the Eyes of Jesus" using the scripture of Jesus healing the woman with the issue of blood.

WOMEN—THROUGH THE EYES OF JESUS
A Sermon Preached by Beth Glick-Rieman
Bethany Theological Seminary Chapel, Oak Brook, Illinois
January 28, 1976

In a day when the notion of equality for women was unheard of and patriarchal structures of society were strong and uncontested by the culture, Jesus' attitude toward women stands as a strong testimony. By word and action he supported the now current surge toward equality of the sexes and the claiming by women of their full personhood and worth. Consistently he pointed women toward the reality of their having been created in the image of God. Consistently he challenged women to explore the meaning of that for their own lives and to act upon it and live it out. As one studies the encounters of Jesus with the women of his day, several major concerns of the modern feminist movement are clearly discernible. Chief among these are the areas of Role Ascriptions and Expectations, Sexuality and Sex, and Women in Ministry.

In the story of Mary and Martha, Jesus speaks loudly and clearly on the subject of Role Ascriptions and Expectations for women. Let us listen to the story as it told in Luke 10.

Now as they went on their way, he entered a village; and a woman named Martha received him into her house. And she had a sister called Mary, who sat at the Lord's feet and listened to his teaching. But Martha was distracted with much serving; and she went to him and said, "Lord, do you not care that my sister has left me to serve alone? Tell her then to help me." But the Lord answered her, "Martha, Martha, you are anxious and troubled about many things; one thing is needful. Mary has chosen the good portion, which shall not be taken away from her." Luke 10:38-42 [14]

Customarily, this story has been taken to mean that it is not good for women to be overly concerned with household duties and chores. It has been accepted in our culture until recently (and in many homes, even now) that household chores and duties are indeed the responsibility of women. This area of life is seen as their domain. Girls are conditioned from early ages to see housekeeping and wifery as a means to their own self-fulfillment. It is the OVER EMPHASIS on this to the neglect of other things that has been thought to be the message the scriptures are giving through this story. I believe that Jesus was saying something quite different than that. When he told Martha that Mary had "chosen the greater portion which shall not be taken away from her," he was saying that to seek truth and to ponder the spiritual, deeper meanings of life is far more important than to prepare and serve food to guests. But he was saying much more than that. He was in effect supporting and encouraging Mary's rebellion against role ascriptions and expectations placed upon her by her society and her sister. He was also pushing back the limited horizons of Martha's vision of herself. He chided her for her preoccupation with things. One cannot hear such admonitions without bringing to mind the image of our capitalist, product-oriented, commercialized society. Every day we are bombarded with the appeal of things. The media have become the channels through which we discover all those things which we need for our happiness, our pleasure, our self-fulfillment. Jesus said, "Martha, you are on the wrong track. Things will not get you to the central meanings of life." Would he not also today condemn the *Total Woman Way* of life that uses people to acquire things and sees the worth of life resting in one's status, looks and possessions? Jesus supported Mary in her inner drive to be more than a "producer or a consumer." And in this act, he demonstrated that the truth is for all who seek it, be they male or female. Through his encouragement of Mary, he claimed for all women the right to be free. Free of role expectations and free for seeking truth, being learners, being channels of God's grace to others. In this act, he declared that women were not created to be put in boxes or surrounded by boundaries. In this act Jesus asserted that no one can deprive women of the God-given power, energy, creativity and hope that comes to them through communion with God. Once that good thing is chosen, it cannot be taken away!

A second major focus of Jesus in his encounters with Women

was that of Sexuality and Sex. As one reads the scriptures, it is apparent that this theme prevailed throughout the life of those people, even as it does today. In that day, as in this, women were viewed as possessions, first of their fathers, later of their husbands. They were relegated to second-class citizenship. Their decisions were not their own. Their bodies were not their own. They were considered unclean and defiled at precisely that time in their lives during which their femaleness and womanhood were most present and inescapable to them. In two different encounters with women, Jesus refused to accept this view of women. You will recall the story of the ruler who came to plead for help for his daughter who had just died. It was as Jesus responded to him that the first of these encounters occurred. Here the story as it is told in Mark 5.

And a great crowd followed him and thronged about him. And there was a woman who had had a flow of blood for twelve years, and who had suffered much under many physicians, and had spent all that she had, and was no better but rather grew worse. She had heard the reports about Jesus, and came up behind him in the crowd and touched his garment. For she said, "If I touch even his garments, I shall be made well." And immediately the hemorrhage ceased; and she felt in her body that she was healed of her disease. And Jesus, perceiving in himself that power had gone from him, immediately turned about in the crowd, and said, "Who touched my garments?" And his disciples said to him, "You see the crowd, pressing around you, and yet you say, 'Who touched me?'" And he looked around to see who had done it. But the woman, knowing what had been done to her, came in fear and trembling and fell down before him, and told him the whole truth. And he said to her, "Daughter, your faith has made you well; go in peace, and be healed of your disease." Mark 5:24-34 [15]

One of the wonders of the scriptures for me is the fact that many passages embody great truths. The picture here is that of a woman who had lived with the degradation and disregard of people for twelve years. She lived under the religious code which is described in full in Leviticus 15:25-28:

If a woman has a discharge of blood for many days, not at the time of her impurity, or if she has a discharge beyond the time of her impurity, all the days of the discharge she shall continue in uncleanness; as in the days of her impurity, she shall be unclean. Every bed on which she lies, all the days of her discharge, shall be to her as the bed of her impurity; and everything on which she sits shall be unclean, as in the uncleanness of her impurity. And whoever touches these things shall be unclean, and shall wash his clothes, and bathe himself in water, and be unclean until the evening. But if she is cleansed of her discharge, she shall count for herself seven days and after that she shall be clean.

It is likely that this woman was a religious woman, believing in the pronouncements of the religious leaders of her day. That burden must have been incredible indeed. And it must have been just that heaviness alongside a great faith and vision of wholeness that prompted her to take the risks of "touching" this man from Galilee who had the reputation of being a healer. I have a hunch that she recoiled in fear and shame when Jesus asked the crowd, "Who touched my garments?" She had violated a man—a teacher—and her punishment might well be severe. Jesus' response to her as she fell in fear and trembling before him must have astounded the religious leaders of his day! He obviously viewed sexuality as central to the wholeness of women. And he recognized in this woman a drive toward wholeness, coupled with a strong faith in the healing power of God. There was no trace of condemnation or disapproval in his voice. There is no evidence of consternation over his having been "defiled" by an unclean woman. Rather, without hesitation he accepted her and affirmed her faith. And he sent her on her way with peace and joy and blessing, restored to full health.

Sexuality as I have used it here refers to the essence, the totality, of being a woman—or a man—the fullness of womanhood and manhood. Not only was sexuality a concern of Jesus. In another instance he confronted directly and unequivocally the whole matter of sex and the sexual practices of his day. Since women were considered to be the possessions of men, they were treated as sex objects for the pleasure of men. The religious laws of the time supported these practices. It is likely that this is the reason that it was used by the Pharisees as a testing point for Jesus, for they were angry with him and confused by his message.

Early in the morning he came again to the temple; all the people came to him, and he sat down and taught them. The scribes and the Pharisees brought a woman who had been caught in adultery and placing her in the midst they said to him, "Teacher, this woman has been caught in the act of adultery. Now in the law Moses commanded us to stone such. What do you say about her?" This they said to test him, that they might have some charge to bring against him. Jesus bent down and wrote with his finger on the ground. And as they continued to ask him, he stood up and said to them, "Let him who is without sin among you be the first to throw a stone at her." And once more he bent down and wrote with his finger on the ground. But when they heard it, they went away, one by one, beginning with the eldest, and Jesus was left alone with the woman standing before him. Jesus looked up and said to her, "Woman, where are they? Has no one condemned you?" She said, "No one, Lord." And Jesus said, "Neither do I condemn you; go, and do not sin again." John 8: 2-11 [16]

I have often wondered what Jesus wrote with his finger on the ground that day—or if he wrote anything. In any case, he gave a strange response to a testing question. The adulterous men had dragged their victim into his presence. And he had quickly perceived their need to absolve their guilt by condemning the woman—the object of their abuse. He was not to be led astray by a question concerning an interpretation of the law of Moses. With sharp insight and rare courage he went straight to the heart of the matter. He put the bee on the guilty ones—not by a judgment but by a question. To the men he said, "Is there any one among you who is not guilty? This woman could not possibly commit adultery alone! Let the innocent one cast the first stone." Well—as snow disappears under the burning rays of the sun, so the men disappeared under the penetrating power of the integrity of Jesus. Only the woman was left—and to her he spoke words not of judgment and condemnation, but of acceptance and support. He said, "I do not condemn you. Go, and never again allow your body to be used or abused by others. You are of great worth. You are a child of God. Live in the power of that knowledge."

A third major concern of feminist church women today—and one to which Jesus spoke by his actions and his words, is that of Women in Ministry. I am here using the term, ministry, to include not only professional pastoral ministry, but also Christian education and all other related ministries.

Jesus must have thought that women were eminently fitted to carry on his work of making known the love and goodness of God. In his parables of the Kingdom, he gave to a woman the God-image.

In this parable Jesus portrays the seeking, caring, active concern of a loving God in the person of a woman. She was a woman of intelligence, resourcefulness, strength, determination and intentionality. She saw that in a very common task there lay the possibilities of joy and discovery. She was not sweeping in order to have a clean house—or a cleaner house than her sister. She was sweeping because she had a vision. Through the use of her energies something that was lost might be restored to full use. A lost coin is worthless. A coin in hand is translatable into power. She is pictured as an agent of redemption. Like God she worked with patience and diligence, refusing to give up until the coin was found. And, like God, she was celebrative and joyous in the realization of a fulfilled hope.

On another occasion, Jesus gave to a woman an important task in ministry. It was in a setting of defiance of the religious do's and don'ts of his day. He had chosen to speak at length and in public, freely and intimately, to a woman—a Samaritan woman at that—whom he had met at a well. And not only did he speak with her. Together they spoke of deeply spiritual and symbolic matters—of living water, of the nature of God as Spirit and Creator, of worship and salvation and truth. She was a very perceptive woman. Listen to a part of their conversation as it is recorded in John.

> *The woman said to him, "Sir, I perceive that you are a prophet. Our fathers worshiped on this mountain; and you say that in Jerusalem is the place where men ought to worship." Jesus said to her, "Woman, believe me, the hour is coming when neither on this mountain nor in Jerusalem, will you worship the Father. You worship what you do not know; we worship what we know, for salvation is from the Jews. But the hour is coming, and now is, when the true worshipers will worship the Father in spirit and truth, for such the Father seeks to worship him. God is spirit, and those who worship him must worship in spirit and truth." The woman said to him, "I know that Messiah is coming (he who is called Christ): when he comes, he will show us all things." Jesus said to her, "I who speak to you am he."*
> John 4: 19-26 [17]

Is it not astonishing indeed in the light of the man-woman relationships of that day that Jesus entrusted such a truth to this woman? Undoubtedly, he recognized in her one who was open to his most important self-revelation. He knew that she would be an active and an insightful agent of his truth to others. He sensed her intelligence, her sharp awareness of the Jewish-Samaritan controversy, her dynamic religious faith and her ability to spread the word. And so he gave to her a most important task in ministry.

The centrality of women in the crucifixion/ resurrection story is a further indication of Jesus' attitudes toward women in ministry. It was women who first discovered that the tomb was empty. It was to women that Jesus first appeared as the Risen One and revealed his intimate relationship with God. It was Mary Magdalene, that woman whose morals were suspect and whose "reputation" was known who believed and testified to the disciples, "I have seen the Lord."

But Mary stood weeping outside the tomb, and as she wept she stooped to look into the tomb; and she saw two angels in white, sitting where the body of Jesus had lain, one at the head and one at the feet. They said to her, "Woman, why are you weeping?" She said to them, "Because they have taken away my Lord, and I do not know where they have laid him." Saying this, she turned around and saw Jesus standing, but she did not know that it was Jesus. Jesus said to her, "Woman, why are you weeping? Whom do you seek?" Supposing him to be the gardener, she said to him, "Sir, if you have carried him away, tell me where you have laid him, and I will take him away." Jesus said to her, "Mary." She turned and said to him in Hebrew, "Rab-bo ni!" (which means Teacher). Jesus said to her, "Do not hold me, for I have not yet ascended to the Father; but go to my brethren and say to them, I am ascending to my Father and your Father, to my God and your God." Mary Magdalene

*went and said to the disciples, "I have seen the Lord";
and she told them that he had said these things to her.*
John 20:11-18 [18]

Yes! It was to women that Jesus first entrusted the Good
News. And it was women who were the first proclaimers, ministers of the Gospel. Truly, Jesus had no problem with giving
women prominent places in his most important ministry to the
world. Indeed, he chose them ahead of men at some of the most
crucial points in that ministry.

The message is clear. When Jesus looked at women, he did
not see dependent, submissive, second-class creatures who
were to be relegated to powerlessness, to be used for men's
purposes and pleasure. NO! He saw full human beings, created in the image of God, destined for wholeness, creativity
and mission. That message is almost 2000 years old! May God
grant us the vision, courage and faith to act upon it in our day!

Ironically, that sermon got me fired from my position on the
staff—well, "not fired, because we have no reason to fire you.
We are letting you go." That was the way "uppity" women were
handled in the late seventies by all-male executive committees
in every field. Joan, a professor friend of mine was "denied
tenure." Several women friends, like me, were "let go" by male
executives restructuring their church positions, as I was.

I quickly learned that it was church women who started the
protest against me. I had "spoken of blood in the pulpit," and
"should be removed from the Brotherhood staff." Even more
painful was the fact that the protest against me was started by a
woman from my home church who wanted my job. And got it.

I was instructed by my boss to appear for a citation at the

following Board meeting. In response I said to him, "I want no citation. As this is the last time I will be attending General Board meetings as a member of the staff, I am asking for time to share some of my thoughts and dreams with you. Instead of the customary citation, please grant me the 10 minutes for such reflection." He granted my request and so I made the following presentation to the Board.

STATEMENT TO GENERAL BOARD
October 24, 1978
Beth Glick-Rieman

As this is the last time I will be attending General Board meetings as a member of the staff, I asked for time to share some of my thoughts and dreams with you. Instead of the customary citation, I have been granted ten minutes for such reflection.

It is my hope that in these moments I can paint a picture of my three years of work as Person Awareness Coordinator and articulate my vision for the church's continuing work in helping persons achieve full personhood and in transforming the systems and structures of church and society.

The Person Awareness Coordinator position was instituted as a staff position in response to the pleas of women for mutuality and equality within the Church of the Brethren. It was built on the premise that oppression, inequalities and abuses do indeed exist and are antithetical to the Spirit of Christ. Furthermore, oppression implicates the oppressors so that both female and male are restricted and denied expression of their full potentiality.

So it was that my task was to enable liberation from the oppressions that happen among us. This was and is a social justice issue and has its counterpart in the biblical message. The Bible is one continual story of God's action in human history to liberate humankind for full and free living. Then, as now, that liberation comes out of pain and struggle. It requires courage, commitment and risk. The way to the Promised Land of freedom requires leaving the safety of Egypt, wandering in a Wilderness of changing values, roles and ways of being, leaving the known and venturing into the risky unknown. For these three years that I have been Person Awareness Coordinator, many of us have been at various stages on our journey out of our Egypts, into the Wilderness, moving toward our Promised Land of fullness of life. We have begun to relinquish our pet theories, our absolute beliefs, our sure faith. We have opened ourselves to the threats of new awareness and responsible uses of new power.

We have seen such a process going on also in the world around us. In Latin America, the poor revolt against the weight of dependency on and exploitation by rich nations and exclusion from a decent standard of living, and ask for independence, self-direction and more of the earth's resources. Underdeveloped nations tire of being the "have-nots" and challenge the "haves." Blacks are naming themselves and redefining their identity. Women everywhere are beginning to refuse the categories and definitions placed upon them by men and stand in their own strength as persons of worth. Such movements bring unrest and upheaval. They uncover anger and hostility. They demand of us a reappraisal of our attitudes and values. It is a time of testing and change, a time of uncertainty and threat.

Just such a time was 1st century A.D. when the man Jesus

challenged existing rules, customs and values to the extent that he has been a central figure in history for almost 2000 years.

Feminist theology, on which the Person Awareness Program has been built, has three major thrusts:

1. Worldviews are in collision
2. We begin at a different starting point
3. We operate out of a different understanding of power and hope

As a Christian feminist, I have called us to move from a hierarchical to a relational worldview. A stair-step mentality with God at the top, then Jesus, then men, then women, then children, then animals and finally plant life has brought our world to the brink of annihilation. In such a view, each above the other is free to dictate, command, use or abuse those beneath. Male/female inequality and imbalance are causal factors for our many symptoms and societal problems. An ecological crisis is worsening; war and violence are rampant; child abuse and wife battering have reached epidemic proportions (yes, in the Church of the Brethren, too), there is rape and incest, hunger, poverty and disease. Might is right and big is good, violence is recreation and killing is entertaining. Goodness is a matter of keeping the rules and love is allowed only under prescribed conditions such as marriage and the family.

As did Jesus, Christian feminists are calling for a radical transformation of the existent social structure within the church and the world. Person Awareness has been asking that these structures be based on mutuality and openness, committed to empowerment of the powerless, recognizing the interdependence of each with all others and all of life—plant, sea and air. In this relational worldview, we insist that women are to be valued and visible. They are encouraged to be responsible, strong, and decisive. Men are capable of tears and deep emotion. They are allowed to be weak and sometimes lacking in judgment. Both are human and fallible. Both together accept the privileges and take the responsibilities to bring about justice, peace and human dignity for all people. Together we must exercise courage and take risks. Children must be valued and nurtured by both parents. Creation is owned by God. All of life is of worth. There are no "more important" categories.

In the second place, I as a feminist begin with a different starting point for moving toward Ultimate Meaning. Doctrines, dogmas and "handed-down" truths to be preserved and learned are no longer the starting point. Rather, we must begin with life experience, the existential reality of oppression, denial, injustice, inequality, and domination. From that starting point I have reflected on the church's participation and complicity in those realities and have called for corrective action according to the Spirit of Christ. I have called for and continue to call for a careful reexamination of the prevailing ideology of domination/subjection between males and females—an oppressive conditioning more pervasive and insidious than any other over centuries of time. From the starting point of our own experience as women, we move to change the classist, racist, economic and ecological exploitation that destroy persons and deny the continuing revelation of God in human history.

Thirdly—Person Awareness—feminist theology—has operated out of a new understanding of power and hope. Hope is present rather than future oriented. The aim is empowerment, not power over. The empowerment of persons in their present oppressive situations (the raising of consciousness, the identification of values, the encouragement of imagination and vision, the calling out of gifts) can and has begun to move persons toward a different kind of future. Persons have been encouraged to act on existing conditions to transform and radicalize their personal lives, the culture, the society and the church. There has been (and must continue to be) insistence on the fact that language is a tool by which we shape reality and new words are needed to articulate new truth. Inclusive language must replace the language of exclusion, invisibility and second-class status of women. I have worked out of the belief that hope and empowerment go hand in hand and that creation is a constant process of renewal from within. I have encouraged us all to move toward changing the repressive patterns of our lives and the oppressive structures so that our future as women and men of the church can be characterized by the biblical concept of shalom—as wholeness, trust and peace. With intentionality, determination, compassion and gratitude I as Person Awareness Coordinator have acted in the belief that a transformed church must be brought into being. I have studied and learned to envision ways of impacting the marketplace, the society and the world toward a fuller humanity, future of promise and hope.

I am grateful for the opportunities of the past three years to serve the General Board as Person Awareness Coordinator. This position has provided me an arena in which to live out the truth as I see it, to actualize some of my dreams for the church that I love, to learn to know sisters and brothers across the country with whom deep sharing of our spiritual journeys was possible. This position has provided a place within the church in which my skills, gifts, and contributions could be used. It has challenged me to grow, to be patient, to be caring, to be knowledgeable. It has encouraged me to test my truth against the community of faith and to act on that truth out of a sense of both justice and mercy. For all of these opportunities I am indeed grateful.

But the task is hardly begun. Our denomination has not yet spoken forthrightly of the oppression of women as an issue of social justice. We have not yet established at the national level a program whose only thrust is advocacy for women. (Such programs have been functioning for as long as 10 years in some denominations). We have resisted change and feared both the process and the future. We have at times acted out of that fear rather than taking the prophetic role of calling ourselves and the church into accountability. We have not yet seen the inescapable connections between women's pain and men's choices. We have not yet affirmed that advocacy for women is a cutting edge of growth for our denomination. We have not yet seen it as the cause underlying such symptoms as broken marriages, child abuse, war, violence, hunger, and pollution. But we have begun to break the conditionings that chain creativity and deny wholeness. We have begun to break the conditions that lead to dependency, competition, jealousy, distrust and woman-as-sex-object mentality.

We are on the move, and in that movement there is Hope. Let us here today forgive each other for the violations we have committed out of our human fallibility and dedicate ourselves to justice, equality and mutuality so that the transforming tale of women can be told. For it is the story of birthing a new creation—a new world where all of life is valued, where all of life is given the opportunity to achieve its full potential, to take its full responsibility and give its gifts, where the boundaries are broken and the chains cast aside and we all walk freely and joyously. May the Spirit of Christ be among us as we continue our task.

My sense of betrayal by the church to which I had been committed since birth was deep and painful. It was no longer an institution "divinely ordained by God." It became a very human institution, peopled by very fallible human beings with power needs of their own. This incident produced in me a lasting crisis in that kind of "blind faith." When I applied for a different job in a different denomination, I was told that it was given to a younger woman, because "You are over-qualified and we would be required to pay you a higher salary."

My disillusionment with the Christian Church and Christianity at large was deepening. I had reached the point where I could not tolerate the dualisms and sexist language of the church. Going to church actually made me sick. I left every service with a headache that lasted the rest of the day. A woodworking nephew created a sign for my wall that read: "Holy Termite." It fit me to a T. I was spending my days eating away at the structures of a "sacred" institution that had shut me out and called me "heretic."

In the fall of 1982 I decided to become a member of the staff of Another Way in San Diego, California. Another Way was a social science organization dedicated to bringing about change in the sexist church and society. Ken Mitchell invited me to join the organization as a team member with him.

Team member Ken Mitchell

Saying "yes" to that invitation was a tremendous leap of faith. I sold my house and my car, got rid of 500 books, and a bunch of household belongings and bought a one-way ticket on Delta, headed for the Franciscan Convent in San Diego, my temporary home. It was to be a whole new life, and it was.

Living with all women was fun at first. I felt accepted by them all. They were kind, warm toward me. About a week after I had been living there, I got awake one morning to an unusual kind of stirring and activity on the part of the nuns. I asked Sister St. George what was going on, as she stood beside a huge box of crucifixes. Other nuns were busy removing all pictures and posters from the walls and replacing them with crucifixes.

"The Bishop is coming today. They will evaluate whether or not we can remain in the Order."

During the Seventies, I spent many long and lonely days and months moving through the stark grief of losing my Peggy and emerging into a new identity apart from "mother." In that process, writing poetry became a healer, a comforter, a creative release.

The poems I include here are an invitation to the reader to walk with me for awhile that hard journey which has no end.

FROM DEATH TO LIFE
Easter morning
On the Fourth Anniversary of Peggy's Burial

Let go, Cold Earth, your hold upon me now.
Death's agony is passed.
The leaf is on the bough.
The roses bloom again.
Free in this moment of the pain and loss,
I know an empty tomb,
The Easter day has triumphed o'er the cross.
The world is new again.
Her world of Spirit blends now with my own,
Invisible and real.
From thence I need not ever walk alone.
Our worlds are one.

5/25/76

REVERIE AT SEASIDE

May 20, 1990

On the 18th Anniversary of Peggy's Burial

Ocean Beach

Sunshine, Warm Sand

Early
I was drawn beside the
  sea
To worship
On this very holy day.

Nearly her lifetime ago
Her lifeboat sailed
over the edge
Beyond the rim
into a world I cannot
  reach.

Her tiny sails
moved
Out of sight
and left me
weeping
on the shore.

And still
today
I sit
and weep
upon the shore.

The wonder
of her life
and mine,
the Mystery
of her death
and mine
call me to worship.

Here I am
in reverence
and awe.

Where
aquamarine deeps
touch
azure sky
out at the rim,
thin streaks
of fragile clouds
go thinning
toward the East.

Abrupt
and clear
As sorrow's

sudden grasp
of teardeeps
in my soul,
so
wind and wave
open white sails
to give and toss
far,
far out on the edge.

Outside church walls
that deprecate her kind,
deny to Goddess Energy
her power to give
and nourish life,
I pause
this sacred moment
Her Spirit
now
to bless
and claim it as my own.

Playing with children
on this edge,
I mark
the coolness
and warmth
of frothing surf.

The lure of tidepools
in the pocked

volcanic rocky shelves
reveal
the tip
of Mother Ocean's secrets.
Hermit crabs know
to take their homes
where'er they go.
A million scurrying
creatures
hide in
amongst
the pinks and greens and
  browns
of billowing seaweed
gracing
every little pool.
A work of art
beyond imagining.

Long time goes by.

I raise again
my gaze
to that far edge
of green and blue.

White sails no more.
Framed now
in perfect stillness
mid the piles
of pier

and reaching
toward the shore
full billowing
redblood sails
send forth
her voice
upon the Spirit Wind.

"I live,"
she said.
"Beyond the rim
of time
and space
and knowing
Beyond the need to prove

or earn
or do,
I live!
It's simply true.

"And not alone
I live.
In spirit worlds
Beyond the need
for knowing
the world is one,
Goddess and God
    together.

"Journey on."

RE-CREATION

O soul of mine,
Pluck from the twisted, broken dreams
Of yesteryear
The memories that beam and bless.

Frame these in gratitude,
And then.
Move fresh, renewed and re-created
Into this new day.

4/23/76

REINCARNATION?

I spoke of immortality—
Of life beyond the grave.

They smiled at me derisively
And said, "You have no proof."
"Believers of the past have had no proof."
"Dismiss it as ridiculous."

I walked away to shed my tears alone.
Dulled, sullen, denied access to my dead.

I found the woods were full of butterflies—
Of teaming life—
Of auburn hair and Peggy's voice.

Then I came back to speak my word once more:
The Spirit broods, creates, renews, incarnates.
Call it what you may.
My dead are living still for me today,
And I shall live eternally—as they

Koinonia Family Reunion

8/4/77

BUTTERFLIES—WE

We are butterflies—
You and I.
Flitting in and out of each other's spaces.
Freely.
Warmed by the sun
Kissed by the rain—
Energized by the breezes that give us life.

You are a Monarch.
Bold colors—orange and black with white.
Beautiful.
You fly rhythmically, gracefully, joyously—loving the
flight and the day in which you fly.
You rest.
You die.
And you emerge from your cocoon.
To fly again—all beautiful and new.
I, too.

We share a world of
Energy!
Joy!
Invitation!
We will not be caged by
Certainties,
Demands,
Or other's flights.

We fly—Free!
We fly
Because we are butterflies
And to fly is to live

8/27/74

DEMONS

Or Angels?
Which is which?
The holy
And unholy
Strive
Within my sea of life
As on a battleground.
Are not the Angels
Only Demons
Claimed
And tamed?

12/15/76

THE POLES

North star
Little dipper
Frigid blue night sky
Above.

Frozen solid earth
Squeaky, snowy footsteps
Underneath.

Framework for time world
Pointers to the timeless

Somewhere
Almost out of reach
Meeting of spirits
Gone
And here
In quiet certainty.

Two poles joined
In celebration.
Racking pain of grief
Ecstasy of reunion

1/26/76

ONCE YOU BROUGHT ME PEACE

In love you shared my burden;
We walked under it together and it did not crush me
I felt able to stand straight.

But then you strode away toward life
to break the spell my burden put upon you.

You left a memory and a hope.
and though it granted no escape
for me, it did increase my
strength to carry on.

Now you've come back—but not to me.

Love bears all things, 'tis said.
But not this time. It is too much
to ask that you should come and
choose its weight again.
And so my burden falls upon me
heavier than before.

For once you brought me peace

7/16/70

WEEP, WOMAN. WEEP!

And let the tears dissolve
your bitterness of soul.

That you may find the self
washed clean and bare
to be that larger self
that is required for
this day's stern demands
of love.

7/13/70

VULNERABLE

Bruised by your tenderness
As rose petals bruise
Earth's deep green carpet
Beneath them.

Blessed by your love
As life-giving air surrounds me,
A delicate pink fragrance
Ever borne along.

11/28/70

REMINDERS

A million snowflakes
Each unlike the other.

A million reminders
Of the infinite variety

Of the universe.

1/23/70

RAINBOW

Fragile and fleeting
You span the darkened skies
As you have spanned the centuries
Of time.

Timeless
In your going
You leave beauty enough
To ponder for a lifetime.

7/23/76

ODE TO A FACULTY MEETING

A cat caught a mouse at the edge of the porch.
I stood there and watched the cruel game.
The cat was in power;
She played by the hour
In pretense and oblivion to pain,
Now giving the mouse almost freedom to run,
Now slapping him back into place.
(And when in the struggle he collapsed and gave up,
She came near and spit in his face.)
Extending—withdrawing—
Pretending—uncaring,
She crushed out his life with great ease,
Then dragged his poor body out into the sunshine
To do with him just as she pleased.

The pain of those moments will not go away.
And it's clear to me why this is true.
(The cat and the mouse are dumb creatures you say,
And know nothing better to do.)

Even so, there's a sadness that stays with me still,
Welling up in great anger and shame.

There are so many humans right there on that porch
Still playing the cat and mouse game.

8/30/74

GOD?

The cardinal sits and sings
Oblivious to the wars beneath her feet.
The pain, the death, the joy, the life.
The cardinal sits and sings.

The seasons come and go.
The people live and die.
The leaders rise and fall.
And Hunger stalks the world.

The cardinal sings on.

Your song, Bird,
When, and how, and why?

Could it be—GOD?

4/6/76

WOMAN

I and my world are one.

I am a woman.
I stand erect, and proud, and free.
I claim my space and power
To be all I can be.

I can give warmth such as the sun has given me.
I can be moving, flowing as the sea.
I can reflect the light as do the moon and myriad stars.
I nourish life and growth as earth has nourished me.

Life-force that pushes seasons in and out now quickens me.
Revolving worlds impinge on mine with energy.
Within myself I sense the wholeness of the world.
Cocoons and shattered egg shells tell my history.

Yes, I am Woman.
Claiming, naming and proclaiming,
Together, in and with my world,
I am complete

9/17/75

MYSTERY

*As the winding road is lost to view
in the early morning fog
which hovers heavily over
hills and valleys,
so the day is veiled in mystery and hiddenness.*

*Love, teach me
not to try to grasp the* coming hours,
*for I cannot know what will be plainly seen
when the sun permeates and the fog lifts.*

*Rather, let me start to walk in faith the pathway
At my feet which now is clear.*

*Mysteries of my tomorrows give courage
to my faltering feet today, through the
love of one whom I have been given to
walk beside me.*

9/28/70

POWER POTENTIAL

WOMAN, minus chains
Multiplied by millions
Equals
>*ENERGY to promote Justice*
>>*TIME to nourish Peace,*
>>>*POWER to banish Poverty,*
>>*DETERMINATION to outlaw Hunger,*
>>*VISION of new worlds*

Where Hope abounds and Truth sets free.
WOMAN POWER,
God-given Power
Shall find RELEASE!

>*(A Paraphrase of Luke 10:38-41)*

>*A sister called Mary sat at the Lord's feet and listened to his teachings. And Jesus said Mary has chosen the good portion which shall not be taken away from her.*

>*You will know the truth, and the truth will make you free.*

>*If the Son, therefore, shall make you free, you shall be free indeed. John 8:36*

9/29/75

AIRBORNE

Up & over the Potomac
Sitting placidly in the midst
Of the sprawling city.
Car bugs grow ever smaller
As we leave them far below creeping along
On ribbons of interstate.
A perfect eight-patterned cloverleaf
Lies still within a green meadow.
Ringed by more busy highway.
Toy houses shaped in blocks
And swirls, triangles, circles, squares
Appear & disappear beneath our feet.
Green wooded hills
Are cut into by red clay fields
Lying mist laden in the early sunshine
The day is not yet full awake.
Clusters of gleaming rooftops
Nest among tree-fringed green meadows.
Propellers roar on through blue haze.
The wooded hulks of mountains
Stand silent sentinel under the slithering snaky Skyline
Drive
And then the Valley floor!
A crazy quilt of luscious farmlands, homes
And rivers, ponds, cornfields, cattle
Day is in full glory
Touching down.

Piedmont 959
D.C. to the Valley
9/20/76

THE OLD DOMINION

We rise again into the morning sky
And below us
Voluptuous, rounded breasts
of Mother Nature
Lie silently
Among the myriad ponds
Of myriad shapes
While early sun rays
Turn the waters
Into mirrors
Flashing through the misty air.
More clouds than sun now
As we move over
Many waters gathered into one
The sun plays hide & seek
Among the clouds
And Nature's artist's brush
Steals golds & pinks
To throw into the waters
Where they gleam & glide
In whimsied play.
The Potomac hugs the
Landing strip
A lone seagull
Flaps wings in fruitless competition

The Capitol
Appears in misty fog
And the runway
Appears beneath us
Just in time.

Piedmont 940
Charlottesville to DC
9/21/76

BREAK FORTH—GO FORTH

Sisters we are.
And sisters we will be

The Spirit moves within us
Impelling us to name ourselves,
Bringing new life into being.

Sisters are we.
And sisters we will be.

The Spirit moves among us,
Urging us to use our power to empower others,
Bringing a new world into being

10/77

IMAGES OF WOMEN

The Church says
Woman, NO !
You may not be this way.
You must be that.
These only are the marks of faithful womanhood.

And I, a woman,
Stand erect in my own strength and say

Build me no boxes,
Lift from me your weights.
Break wide your boundaries.
Cast from me your chains!

God's invitation comes to me
Direct and clear,
Through Christ,
It is to Freedom, Love,
Wholeness and Power.

And I say YES !

1978

THE ABBEY OF ST. NORBERT

The Abbey sat there in the low grass,
Calm and still,
Empty

And ready to be impregnated
With the seedlings of new growth
For those of us who came.

Surrounded
And permeated by the silences
Of souls come and gone,
And seasons pausing, rolling on,
The driftwood Christ with arms upheld
Saying no word,
The Roman candle burning in the midst.

We brought our sounds
Of laughter and of pain,
Of demons on the run,
Of celebration.

And heavy, patriarchal forms
And unborn creativity
Creaked and cracked open
At the hands of Love.

The Abbey sits there still in the low grass,
Calm and still.
We have passed on.

The Abbey now is Holy Ground for us,
Emblem of Hope.
The bells speak with many voices.

10/28/78

LOVE OF LIFE

My love of life is
Many loves
Rolled into one.

Storm clouds and rain, the rainbow and the sun,
Tender green grass alive beneath my feet
The thrill of flying skyward, fast and fleet
A fountain gushing—swishing, swirling on
The plaintive call of mourning doves at dawn.

The Stars and Stripes' surrender to the breeze
A busy young child playing round my knees
The wonder of a far-off shooting star
The sweetness of a nutty chocolate bar

Laughter and tears, smiles, frowns,
The cold and warm
Display of heavenly fireworks in a storm
The power to think and reason, touch and feel
Delicious, varied tastes of many a meal.

Brisk winds of winter, squeaky ice and snow
The changing scenes as on through life I go
The reds and golds and rusts of chilly fall
Low shrubs and towering trees, the small and tall.

Renewing, re-creating powers of rest
The love of friends and those who know me best
And more than all else, moving in my soul
A unity with all
I am a woman—whole.

I did not know in the closing of the seventies that a shock of even greater proportions awaited me, as a new decade opened in my life.

Eight

THE ACHING, EXPANDING EIGHTIES

The Last Embrace—Glenn and Beth

Life seeks to expand in unknown directions for unknown reasons. There is a driving force behind a mystery that we cannot understand, and it includes more than reason alone. The urge to cosmic heroism, then, is sacred and mysterious and not to be neatly ordered and rationalized by science and secularism. …We can conclude that a project as grand as the scientific-mythical construction of victory over human limitations is not something that can be programmed by science. Even more, it comes from the vital energies of masses sweating within the nightmare of creation— and it is not even in our hands to program. Who knows what form the forward momentum of life will take in the time ahead or what use it will make of our anguished searching. The most that any one of us can seem to do is to fashion something—an object or ourselves- and drop it into the confusion, make an offering of it, so to speak, to the life force.[19]

The decade of the 80's was expansive on all fronts, national, international and personal. It began with an emotional shock. My beloved Glenn died. His death changed my identity from loved and treasured wife to stunned and bereaved widow.

It had begun ten years before when Glenn had undergone two major heart attacks, each of which had left him increasingly debilitated. A third, (and fatal) one was in the making.

It was golden October once again, and the air began to have the sting of fall and winter. October 30, 1980—it was time to put away the yard and garden, rake the leaves and pile them into sacks to be taken away.

Halloween was upon us. All Hallows' Eve, October 30, 1980, a Holy night of transformation. One minute I was a beloved wife. The next, at 10 minutes after midnight, I was a widow. Heartbroken. Stunned. In shock. Afraid of the unknown future. Bitterly alone. He had held me in his arms that afternoon and told me that he loved me, and I wept.

"I cannot live without you, Glenn." He held me closer, tenderly.

"You are a strong woman, Beth. You will have many lives to live after I am gone." We held each other, wordlessly, weeping together. He was strengthened for his task of dying, and I for my task of living on to create a fulfilling life without him.

He brought a chair and sat watching as I worked in the yard. He was too fragile to join me. We both knew that we were close to the thin veil that separates life and death. I cooked his favorite meal: mustard greens and potatoes in their skins. He ate a small portion, and thanked me for cooking. We talked about the events of his life that I wanted to include in a book I was planning to write.

That book was never written. Round about 10:00 PM, he said, "I think we need to go to the hospital, Beth. This pain is getting worse." The siren awakened the neighborhood. I held his hand as we drove the seven miles to Rockingham Memorial Hospital in Harrisonburg, praying all the while. Hoping. Fearing the worst. I wanted to stay with him in the emergency room, hesitating when the doctor asked me to go. The doctor actually put his hands on my shoulders and put me out of the room. At 12:10 that same doctor appeared at the waiting room door and said simply. "I'm sorry, but we could not save him. You may come in for a few minutes. What funeral home shall we call?"

It was all so ordinary, like talking about the weather. I called my dear friend Shirley, asking her to take me home. When she left, I tried to call Jill, Marta and Eric. I couldn't reach anyone, so I went to bed weeping. I slept, aware of being on a long journey, ALONE. It was unreal, and it was true. I was a widow at 58.

He was gone forever. I called that moment, and the days and years to follow, another "crack in my cosmic egg."

Gone was the sweet comfort of being loved by one good man, of being a woman who thought of herself as having free choice, privilege.

That long and bitter period of bereavement called up my creative spirit. I wrote the book: *Peggy: I May Not Have the Summer* and merged the two hardest griefs of my life—that of my beloved Glenn and my daughter Peggy—in journal entries that saved my life. I enclose a portion of that book in Appendix A.

"Grief is a wound that needs attention in order to heal," says Tatelbaum in her book, *The Courage to Grieve.* The wounding that happens at the death of a husband and child is searing and deep. Paying attention to that wound is a painful and exhausting process. Working through that kind of grief requires time, and demands a willingness to allow the intensity of feelings to be recognized and released, not once, but over and over again.

The pain was so severe that I wanted to run away from it, to deny it, to rationalize it away, to pretend that "letting go" would heal the wound. I often found myself traveling the dead-end street of comparison. "The Smiths have had so much more to bear than I." I was encouraged in this pretense and rationalization by societal messages that come in myriads of ways. Grieving people are considered a blight, a nuisance, weaklings who cannot accept life's traumas and move on. I sometimes had the feeling that my presence was an embarrassment, a drag on everybody. Like the ancient Hebrew worlds, society does not want to see or respond to grieving people. We "hide our faces from them," (Isaiah 53:3). We hope they will just go away.

Tatelbaum observed:

> *Our society mistakenly values restraint; we risk the*

rejection of others by being open or different...by being willing to journey into pain and sorrow and anger in order to heal and recover.

These attitudes amplified my distress, exacerbated my loneliness. They made it hard for me to believe that healing is possible. They encouraged me to distrust my intuition, my strength and my faith in the future. They pushed me towards losing heart, rather than acting with courage.

Grievers get the message that we are to move on, and quickly. We are not to "dwell on it," or to "get stuck" in tears and self-pity. The living don't want to be reminded that death cannot be avoided, that the "Grim Reaper" stands in the wings with his scythe, ever ready at any moment to cut us down, one by one.

Attitudes toward people in grief are intricately intertwined with attitudes toward death. Grief reminds us that death is an inevitable, inescapable part of life. We are a mixed up and violent society, and our beliefs about death are convoluted, and contradictory. On the one hand, death is considered "the enemy." Youth is valued above old age; dying is regarded as ugly and to be avoided as long as possible. We act like teen-agers who think we have a right to live forever, that death has no "right" to be interrupting the flow of our living, that terminal disease is not "fair." This sense of "death as the enemy" is particularly strong at the death of the young. It is voiced in comments like "How could a good God let this happen?" or "It isn't fair!" Deep in our psyches we have internalized the message that we are to avoid death at all costs.

So, we engage in all sorts of behaviors to deny aging and prolong life. Doctors take the Hippocratic Oath declaring that they will do all in their power to keep people alive. Funeral directors work hard to make the dead person look "natural." They cover the excess dirt of a grave site with fake grass and flowers. "Staying young" is a mega-business that takes and makes millions of dollars every year. Getting old is ridiculed, joked about as if it were something we should be ashamed of, or at least be able to choose or not choose. Since aging leads to death, we get the impression that we are not "permitted" to get old, so after 40, we are encouraged to lie about our age. This is especially true for women, who are somehow considered undesirable because they have wrinkles or gray hair or age spots on their skin.

On the other hand, we line the coffers of attorneys to make legal our right to die. If we talk about death and dying, we are thought to be morbid or depressed. Yet, we declare that dying should be a matter of personal choice. We make laws that make such dying illegal. We put doctors in jail for helping people to carry through on that choice.

At the root of our mixed up emotions about death, there is the fear of the unknown that all of us will be called on to face at some point in our lives. Grieving people make us feel helpless in the face of our own mortality. We cannot know what lies ahead, and to be with others in grief and pain accentuates our own sense of helplessness. We are fed this fear of death daily. Terrorists stalk our everyday lives. We take pills and more pills to stay alive. We spend billions preparing vaccines to combat flu. Governments fight wars over their fears of other "nations" real or imagined "weapons of mass destruction."

Every day we are jarred to the core by some gruesome pictures of dying, dying, and more dying. Casualties from the wars in Iraq and Afghanistan mount steadily. We divide the people and nations of the world into two parts, enemies and friends. Suicide bombers die because they are "called" by the God of their religion to eradicate those whom they perceive to be "the enemy"; or perhaps they value killing and dying above living their own lives.

Newspapers, TV newscasts, and countless appeals for money bring us face to face with millions who are dying. Children dying of disease and starvation in every country of the world, including our own rich nation. Death has become so common and everyday that some people have chosen not to read the papers or listen to the news. They cannot bear to feel the helplessness and hopelessness of being unable to do anything about this horrendous situation.

On a personal level, this withdrawal leads to apathy, which leads to inaction, which leads to depression, which leads to withdrawal in an ever-escalating cycle. We live every day with the specter of our own death.

For grieving to be less painful, violence and fear need to be displaced in our minds and attitudes by goodwill and trust. The categories of "Enemies" and "Allies" need to be transformed into "One Family, One World."

Whatever we believe about heaven or hell or the "hereafter," Death comes as transformation, as moving from one plane of existence to another, as a release from bodies that no longer bring pleasure, as freedom from physical pain and debilitation. If death could be seen, not as the enemy, but as the natural and good culmination of a personal lifespan, it would be easier to move through the struggles and loneliness of deep grieving, to open ourselves generously and feel the pain and sorrow of great loss.

Grieving takes a certain courage, a strength of "heart", a determination to claim our right to grieve. It takes a deep, inner sense of oneself, a strong affirmation of the holiness of one's own life experience and that of every other. It takes the will to do our grieving at our own pace. It takes thinking of the careless remarks or advice on "where we should be" as stepping stones to learning where and with whom it is "safe" to let our grief show. It takes knowing that it is not safe everywhere and with just anyone.

So why, if it's so hard, why go through all the pain? Why not just "go on" as so many do, resigned and resolute to what is? Why not avoid it as much as possible? Why not live around it, rather than go through it?

Good grieving brings amazing rewards. Going through it brings us out on the other side as different people. People whose compassion is enlarged, whose understanding is expanded, whose joy is full. In his book *The Prophet,* the poet Kahlil Gibran said,

> *Your joy is your sorrow unmasked. And the selfsame well from which your laughter rises was oftentimes filled with your tears.... The deeper that sorrow carves into your being, the more joy you can contain.*

I know this to be true. The knife that carved my grief has been sharp and unyielding. Yet the underside of that pain and sorrow is the immensity of joy and blessing I experience as a result of the gifts Glenn and Peggy brought to my life. My heart is bigger than before they died; my understanding more true. I am a better person, happier, too, than if I were locked into resentments, bitterness, unresolved pain and an unforgiving spirit.

Good grieving demands that we discover where and with whom to reveal the depths of our pain and anguish. To grieve well requires attention to our wounds, never to exacerbate the pain by expressing it in those places and with those people who cannot understand and empathize.

Good grieving requires of us that we become self-aware, knowing when we are sinking into self-pity, when we are allowing our loss to dominate our living. Good grieving means we know when it is time to be comforted and accepting of death and the loss of the future with that loved person. Good grieving means that we can allow the pain to be there without collapsing into emotional pits of despair and bitterness. There is a delicate balance between living into the depths of the pain and allowing acceptance and healing to move us to a new place. Little by little, we sense in ourselves a softening of the anguish, and a sense of gratitude for the learnings that come through grieving. Good grieving means that we begin to gather to ourselves the blessings and gifts brought by the one who is now absent from us. Grieving is a great Healer.

Tatelbaum says in *The Courage to Grieve* that successful grieving is a three-step process:

First, it is fully experiencing and expressing all
the emotions and reactions to the loss. Second, it is
completing and letting go of your attachment both to
the deceased and to sorrow. Third it is recovering and
reinvesting anew in one's own life.

To miss any one of these stages is to result in incomplete and unsatisfying living. To engage in any one of them requires courage and a strong support group. It also requires the use of tools and rituals that take time. It demands that we give loving attention to the flow of our daily living. Good grieving is a time of personal transformation, yes, even in the midst of pain and anguish. Grieving well is challenging, indeed necessary, for mental and physical health. Acting on the courage to grieve brings rewards that lead to an open and joyous future.

Many "tools" were available to me in my grieving process, and I used them all: weeping, dancing, writing, creating, gardening, listening. Possibly the most valuable tool of all was the use of a journal. I poured hours and hours onto blank pages that served as a release for tears and pain. The act of putting into words a flow of consciousness brought increased awareness of the healing and renewal that are made possible through reflective meditation. The very act of putting pen to paper eased that sense of helplessness which is so engulfing in the face of death. Writing the story over and over released new energies and brought hope and anticipation for the unknown future.

On the political scene, after the perceived failure of Jimmy Carter as president, the people elected Republican Ronald Reagan, and he quickly became popular with millions. I was not among them. He was an arch conservative who favored the wealthy and cut programs for the needy. It grieved me deeply that in his eight years in office the gap between the rich and the poor widened perceptibly. A class called "yuppies" emerged, young adults whose primary motivation was to "get rich quick." Millionaires multiplied and the poor sank even further into misery. On the bright side, relations with Russia were eased. Perestroika and Glasnost under the direction of Mikhail Gorbachev's reforms, coupled with Reagan's willingness to meet with him in summits to negotiate dismantling our two nations' stockpiles of nuclear weapons, led to his declaring that "Russia as an evil empire is no longer true." Suddenly, Russian music was in the air, and Russian composers were honored and played. Student exchanges and trade with Russian companies became common.

I was sad, and very concerned, when Reagan appointed several conservative justices to the Supreme Court. At the same time, his actions to decrease government spending and cut taxes led to his easy victory over Democrat Walter Mondale in 1984. He was known as "The Great Communicator" at the height of his popularity. When he defied Congress and was implicated in exchanging arms for hostages in Nicaragua (The Iran-Contra Affair), and then advocated the SDI missile defense program, he raised both my concerns and international tensions.

It was the time of Aids, and the War on Drugs. Personal computers became common; the Exxon-Valdez Oil Spill and the tragic explosion of NASA"s space shuttle, Challenger, shocked me and the nation and fueled my determination to get more women in positions of decision making and power in government, church and the public sphere. Reagan's friendship with Gorbachev gave me hope. There was a sense of optimism in the air, alongside apprehension toward governmental actions.

On the personal "stage" of my life, my children, now grown to adulthood, were busy expanding the family circle. Because women (I among them) were being ordained as ministers and priests), I was chosen to officiate at a serenely beautiful wedding in North Manchester, Indiana, as Jill Christine and Robert Alan Klingler married on May 28, 1978.

We were thrilled to become grandparents when Daniel Glenn arrived on March 12, 1980, followed by three other small Rieman-Klinglers who widened the boundaries of the family: Joseph David on May 28,1983; John Robert on March 28, 1987; and Maria Christine on October 13, 1990.

The Families Expand!

At the same time, Marta brought Bartholomew Allen Clayton into the family in a Quaker wedding in Xenia, Ohio. They then produced three tiny girls sprinkled in among those grandboys. Tacey Rieman Clayton was born on February 12, 1984. Emma Clayton Rieman came along on December 3, 1987, and Grace Rieman Clayton brought up the rear on September 19, 1990.

Eric, like his father before him, was a late bloomer, still single. It was years later, in 2001, that he brought Jennifer Denise Gall on family stage in Mendocino, California on foggy cliffs above the roaring Pacific. Again, it was no small satisfaction to me, that I, as an ordained woman, was chosen to officiate at the ceremony we three created together. And no small joy for me, on September 10, 2002 to expand the family circle to welcome Zealin Glenn Gall Glickrieman, and on July 13, 2006, Arrow Dwight Gall Glickrieman to round out the grandchildren to nine. Five girls and four boys—amazing! In place of the immense burden of being WIDOW, I was given the joys of grandmothering and burgeoning new life.

Looking back at who I became and how I responded to living my sixties as a single woman, I see a strange dichotomy. On the one hand, profound sorrow rested in every pore of my being. On the other, the capacity of the human creature to heal and move on into creative and generative living was manifested in every decision I made and in all my everyday actions.

Being fired from my job in 1978 had freed me to create my own business which I called "HEIRS: Human Empowerment In Religion and Society." I decided I would dedicate my energies to changing the lives of women and girls toward wholeness and equality in their relationships with men, in their private and public life. It was, I was to learn later, a drop in the bucket of what was happening to women and girls worldwide.

In the name of HEIRS, I built on the contacts I had made as Person Awareness Coordinator and the skills I had gained in the ACC in personal and group development and conflict management. I focused on empowering women in church and society to name and give their gifts, rather than take the position of "submissive helpmate" operating always as if men's judgments (especially husbands) were superior to their own. I had lived in that box for a lot of years of my life, and I saw how diminished and eroded it had made me feel. Very soon, as I led workshops and theological happenings all over the U.S., I learned that men, too, are deprived of their wholeness in a patriarchal society, though surely not as severely as women. I began to include them in my workshops and learning events, which actually were focused on personal and spiritual growth and healthy conflict management between men and women at home and in work and church settings.

Ironically, Glenn's death on October 31, 1980, and an empty nest, opened the door for me to be free to travel and give leadership in workshops and speaking events all over the place.

In 1983 I sold my house and car in the little village of Bridgewater, left the sibling family, and moved to San Diego to join Another Way, the business created by Ken Mitchell. It was an organization whose stated mission matched my own. As team leaders Ken and I created a series of workshops called "Caring Ministry," which we led in many Protestant denominations all over the United States and Canada. HEIRS and ANOTHER WAY became a team with considerable influence in many denominations, a force for changing the lives of people and patriarchal systems that denied wholeness to both women and men.

Beth with her San Diego support group,
Fr. Bill, Sister Bridget, Tiffanee, Carol, and Carl.
Ken Mitchell not shown.

At the same time, HEIRS became known beyond national borders for my work in bringing about the personal growth and leadership of women. A lot of small moments stand out in my memory as I was invited and traveled widely to achieve that goal. I lived through the decade of the 80's with a paradoxical sense of my life having reached a fullness and purpose not known heretofore. My active life led to a fullness of purpose that comforted me, and eased the pain of loss. Those were times of challenge and great joy.

In those grieving eighties and nineties, I was often asked to preach on Sunday mornings that followed a weekend workshop, the topic chosen by the group that had invited me. They were always focused on some aspect of personal growth or conflict resolution.

One such Sunday morning stands out in my memory. It was October 10, 1993, in Edinburgh, Scotland. I was standing in line with the all-male, robed leaders waiting for the pipe organ to give us the cue to process to the front of the church. I suddenly heard a voice saying "Beth, who do you think you are? What on earth are you doing here?"

Without a moment's hesitation, my inner voice responded: "I am here to embody the Divine Feminine, to put a chink in the patriarchal wall of centuries."

The organ sounded and we moved to take our places in the chancel. A short while later, I preached a sermon which I called "Going to the Roots." It is based on three scripture passages that have CHOICE at the heart. (See Appendix B.)

I have often wondered what price Rector Jim had to pay for giving me such a privilege, of taking the risk to act out the truth that had set me free.

A moment, indelible in my memory, happened on my second day in Edinburgh, as I was leading a workshop for a women's group in that church.

I had just said "good morning" to the group when a feisty sister with a pronounced Scottish brogue I could hardly understand, held up a bottle of Scotch and said in a voice everyone could hear:

"Beth, I brought my Scotch along just in case I need a shot when you ask us to share all this personal stuff!"

She brought down the house, having no idea that she was talking to a little "teetotaler" from the rural Shenandoah Valley of Virginia! I recovered my equilibrium as she took a swig, then passed the bottle around. Almost everyone imbibed, everyone except me. After all, I was the leader for the day and I knew my limits where Scotch was concerned. It was a jolly group. I had very little tension with which to deal that day!

Another day, my arrival in Bangalore, India, was a series of teaching moments. When I descended from the plane expecting to be met by my good friends with white faces, I joined a sea of brown, not a white among them. In that instant I knew at the gut level what it is to be a minority. A minute later, when an over-eager coolie grabbed my backpack and took off running with me in pursuit to grab it back, I learned what it means to be illiterate. I couldn't understand a word he said! He couldn't understand a word I said. (I got it back!) Thank goodness I had my destination in writing in order to make it understandable to the rickshaw driver. As it was, he wanted to put me off in several places that did not match what was on the card. When it finally did and he had unloaded my luggage, my heart skipped a beat, as he started to move away and the host of the continuing education center came shouting and running for him to stop. It seems my friends had left there the day before and were now at university housing in Bangalore. The driver understood, reloaded and we headed back toward town. I learned to trust those who speak a different language.

Meanwhile, my anxieties were working overtime. What to do? Fly back to San Diego? Never! Go home without seeing India? I would stay and search for my friends and I'd never trust cable again!

What a welcome sight an hour later, when the rickshaw pulled up and stopped at a place where four white faces beamed a welcome. I paid the driver double, he unloaded my luggage and pulled away.

"Donna, Tiffanee, Gavin, and Galen," I screamed, "where's Tim?"

"He's on his way to pick you up at the airport," Donna said. "We got your cable an hour ago."

Tim and Donna Scorer

It was a joyous reunion, followed by a week of sights and sounds and life of a completely different people and culture. We visited ancient holy places, scrambled through halls and climbed time-worn steps of Borodapur, and felt the vibrations of long gone pilgrims seeking the meaning of life in their own time. We spent hours listening to the Gamelon with their clanging cymbals and resounding drums. We shared conversations with people who had spent sabbatical time in the U.S. We were told that "you waste more food at every meal that we have to begin with."

In the wilds of India's Bengal tigers reserve, we slept in a hut overtop a salt lick visited in the middle of the night by elegant wild beasts rummaging about below us. Earlier in the day, all six of us had piled into a jeep made for two and had driven through a forest fire licking and sputtering over grasslands that were dry and scary. Our host was Bishou, an attorney working with the native people who had been displaced to make way for the tigers. He had obtained permission for us to go deep into the area to see those who had been removed from their mud huts and forced onto unfamiliar territory by the government. A small child slept peacefully on the grass outside one hut. Another, about two years old, took a look at my white face, screamed, and ran and hid in her mother's skirts. Their only water supply was the small stream about a stone's throw away. There was no electricity. The village shared a central "cooking hut." I felt as though I had suddenly gone back in time countless years.

In 1990 I joined the estimated 70,000 women who spent a week in Kenya, Africa, attending the Second United Nations World Conference on Women. There, I was confronted with the reality of the way the world views my own United States of America. There were marches against what was perceived as our "Imperialism" our domination of developing countries. There were signs that read "Stop the US. No more aggression!" I thought to myself, "We as a nation are going to get it one of these days. I don't know how it will come, but the world will not long put up with what they judge to be our "unfair use of power."

At that conference, issues affecting the lives of women worldwide, were dealt with in one workshop after another. And I felt encouragement and hope as I saw women rising up all over the world to confront that inequality and abuse, to change the injustices under which they lived.

Following the Conference, I joined a group of women who went on an educational safari westward into wild animal country. At Lake Victoria, we had the breathtaking experience of watching thousands of black-bellied pink flamingos take to the air in one amazing moment. Later, standing on the border between Kenya and Tanzania, we paused in wonder as hundreds of stately, and orderly wildebeests marched head to tail in their annual migration across the wide Serengeti Plain.

For me it was a remarkable time of productivity and personal work life. I spent many satisfying weeks in Naramata Center, British Columbia, a continuing education center of The Church of Canada. There, for several years in a row I led or co-led a three-month residential workshop in personal growth and leadership development for 18–24 year olds. It was called "Winter Session." The feats that age group attempted—and sometimes achieved—made me think they thought they would live forever!

Naramata was sacred ground for me, during the time I spent there, and now as I remember. The lake and surrounding hills were a place of beauty and inspiration. My work with the people there was challenging and satisfying. Like the roses that bloomed in all the corners of the campus, I felt the encouragement of light and love that called me to open to fullness and maturity in leadership unlike anything I had known before.

I was treated like a professional, paid well, and recognized as a skilled and wanted leader. What a difference that made to me as leader! I was never anxious or uneasy in leading groups there. I blossomed under the expectations or others' expectations that their own lives would be enriched when they took the workshops I led.

18–24 year old women participating in a workshop

Looking back now, I think of the place and the people as transformative, precious and lasting. At many places in the US, I as leader felt the need to prove myself, to look good and to assert my knowledge and authority, to be adequate to whatever situation presented itself. Not so at Naramata.

Naramata called out the best in me. I am still thankful that I was invited many times during the 80's and 90's to give leadership there. Of all my far travels and leadership in the US, Scotland, Germany, India, Australia, and Canada, Naramata stands out as special.

My move from San Diego to the East Bay area of San Francisco in 2001, opened up for me the chance to participate as a member of the United Nations East Bay Chapter on the Board of Directors. As an active member of that Board, I had great satisfaction in chairing the UNA Center Committee in charge of the gift shop. We made known, in schools and the community, the work of the United Nations Association worldwide. Our motto was "Think Globally; Act Locally." We worked in many different venues to achieve the Millennium Goals of Equality, Development, and Peace, created by the United Nations World conference on Women in Beijing, China. It was a heady experience to be working with others who were dedicated to improving the lives of women and girls, as I was. From August 2004 through December 2008, I experienced real satisfaction continuing my work with others in actions leading to changing those injustices and abuse.

It was a sad day for me in December, 2008, when a white male became president of the Board and instituted a policy of operation that I felt denigrated and discouraged the contributions of older women in board meetings. I told him so, and realized he was clueless. With regrets, and in protest, I resigned and left the Board. No wonder the nations of the world have trouble maintaining respect for each other!

As the seventies' women's awareness and rage spilled over into the eighties (as the decades always do), branches of "Radical Women" sprang up in city after city across the nation. Realizing the value of combining forces in order to bring about the changes we wanted in society's treatment of women, Radical Women co-sponsored a conference with the Socialist Feminist Movement held in Seattle. I attended that conference as a representative of the church's work on the role and status of women at the national level. In that capacity, I gave a workshop that focused on marriage and divorce, equality and injustice. I addressed the conference on the theme, "Sexuality, Sex, and Survival, A New Look at Intimacy, Alternative Views of Marriage." I was serving on a national study committee of the Church of the Brethren with that assignment at that time. This address was later published in *The Journal of Applied Behavioral Science.*

That conference in Seattle covered many issues facing women in the 80's: Lesbianism, the rising divorce rate, inequality in income, and power in decision-making, rape, wife-battering, incest and on and on.

Ironically, because Ronald Reagan had taken over the White House and Reaganomics had instituted a plan to lower government spending by cutting social programs and taxes, he reduced regulations on industry and the environment. A high percentage of social programs exist for the benefit of women, children and the poor. Reagan's policies benefited the rich and punished the needy; in effect, it widened the already wide gap between the rich and the poor in our society. While a lot of people prospered and Reagan's approval ratings were at an all-time high, women like me cried into our teacups. To make matters worse, Reagan appointed several conservative justices to the Supreme Court. No hope for passing the ERA there. Lots of hope for "The Great Communicator "winning the 1984 election, which he did easily. Then followed the scandal of the Iran-Contra Affair and the secret arms for hostages deal, aiding the Nicaraguan contras which was forbidden by Congress in 1984. What had happened to our democracy, our integrity of public officials?, I wondered.

We were saved by the coming into power in the Soviet Union of the reformer, Mikhail Gorbachev. He had softened

Reagan's anti-Communist stance and inspired the collapse of the Soviet Union. Because the two leaders held summits where they worked on arms control agreements and formed a friendship, Reagan declared an end to the Cold War. I was greatly heartened by the power of the two working together for peace! In 1989, Gorbachev's reforms enabled country after country of the Eastern Soviet Block of the Soviet Union to secede and assert their independence from Communism and their allegiance to democratic forms of government. In the same year, the Berlin Wall separating East and West Germany collapsed, and the rumblings from that historic event stirred hope in me that some advances for women, including the passage of the Equal Rights Amendment, could happen in my own America. The ERA, in full, reads as follows:

Equality of rights under the law shall not be denied or abridged by the United States or by any State on account of sex. Men and women shall have equal rights throughout the United States and every place subject to its jurisdiction.

Even though it seems simple and forthright, it has not been ratified and become the law of the land.

Instead, the first few cases of Aids among homosexual men, focused the attention of the nation on the gay lifestyle. In 1986 President and Nancy Reagan announced a new anti-drug campaign with the slogan "Just Say NO" to the use of illegal drugs. That same year, the tragic explosion of the space shuttle *Challenger,* killing all seven astronauts aboard, shook our confidence in NASA. In March, 1989 the Exxon-Valdez ran aground in Alaska, causing enormous damage to wildlife there and focusing attention on the potential of the oil industry to wreak environmental havoc and destruction. In 1991, the debut of the IBM PC computers was having a profound effect on both the workplace and the society. With all that going on, it felt to me as if women's issues were put on the back burner.

The 80's spilled over into the decade of the 90's and Bill Clinton won the White House in 1992. He began two terms of a very troubled presidency. His lurid personal affair with Monica Lewinsky created a more lurid attempt on the part of the GOP to spend untold energy and hours to impeach him. But a lot of people were prospering during the nineties, and the two-thirds of the Senate needed to remove him from office failed. Ross Perot's Reform Party and Jesse Ventura's election as governor of Minnesota said a mouthful about voter discontent. All of Eastern Europe was in the throes of gaining freedom from Soviet domination. Violence broke out in many places: The collapse of Yugoslavia started a wave of terror in Bosnia. A religious cult called the Branch Davidians killed 75 men, women and children in the Waco disaster in Texas. The militia movement claimed to have fifteen thousand members in forty states, all disenchanted with the perceived governmental abuse of power. Timothy McVeigh, one of these, killed 168 people by bombing the Alfred P. Murrow Federal Building in Oklahoma City in April, 1995. Within two years, five different mass shootings broke out on school grounds across the nation.

The Senate hearings on the nomination of Clarence Thomas to the Supreme Court brought sexual harassment of women into the public eye. Anita Hill had accused him of harassment two years earlier. When Rodney King was severely beaten by police officers, and it was caught on video and the police officers were acquitted, the worst riots in US history erupted in Los Angeles. Racial discrimination became clear to everyone. The rise in violence in America, coupled with the loss of privacy due to technology (The Worldwide Web) were very unsettling for me.

There was one very bright spot. In 1997 the singer, Sarah McLachlan produced the first ever all female Lilith Fair. Women rockers grossed $16 million in 38 shows.

Scientists were excited about the Human Genome Project which mapped the human DNA, claiming fifty to one hundred thousand genes which would revolutionize medicine. Cloning was successful when Dolly was created. Gore brought the plight of the environment to center stage. Issues of processed food and biotechnology began to trouble both activists and ordinary citizens. Studies were done linking diet and disease. Dissatisfaction with the educational system of the country occupied the minds of school teachers and administrators. It was a yeasty, issue- centered time of change.

I could never have imagined how my own life expanded during the decade of the 80's and 90's. Rumblings toward change had been in the making of my activities for decades. Glenn's death, bitterly, had smashed open for me the protective cocoon of marriage. It required of me that I step out of the secure past into the vast and frightening freedom of the largely unknown wider world.

The 90's opened up for me my dream of being on the faculty of a seminary. I was becoming known as a leader on the national scene of The Church of the Brethren. Bethany Seminary in Chicago advertised a position for a professor in Christian Education. I jumped at it. It would give me a platform for letting students know about the horrific situation with girls and women worldwide. I sent in my application, not knowing that the cards were stacked against me. Just a month earlier, the dean who would make the decision, and I, were serving on the program planning committee for the National Youth Conference. He had made numerous sexual innuendos to young girls on the committee, and was flagrantly violating the Ministerial Code of Ethics of the Seminary. He became irate at me when I called attention to it. At one point, he actually touched one girl provocatively, and I said, "Hands off, G!" He looked straight at me and said "Unless or until you get with mainstream thinking, you'll not get a job at Bethany, as long as I'm around there." I never got the job. I learned many years later that he was, at that time, engaged in an illicit affair with a married staff member on the faculty.

"Mainstream," in the late eighties and all through the 1990's was the era of "free love," "open marriage," and the loosening of vows and commitments. Many a fly was zipped open in the wee hours following long day sessions on personal growth in "Spiritual Life Institutes" all across the country. Meanwhile, wives back home with the kids were being "the mothers God intended them to be" proud of their righteous church-leader husbands out there doing "God's work" in a needy world.

And in the overseeing halls of administrative acumen, a great system of "keep it quiet" was put into play. Women, including Shirley and I, were outraged at the whole rotten thing and used our voices in protest. In response, the Ministerial Ethics Committee of Chicago Theological Seminary and several others, slapped the hands of G.S. (and several others). They were put on probation and could not accept leadership at events to which they were invited during the nineties. Big deal. G.S. is still giving leadership in unsuspecting places now, these fifteen years later!

My innocent understanding of the church as a divine institution ordained of God (whose God?) reached an all-time, bitter, disillusioned low. Male power over women's lives, and the abuse and injustice therein became a gut-level lived reality.

I was astounded to discover that most of the world's women and girls live daily under unbelievable abuse, injustice, and downright inhumane conditions. I became aware that at its very roots, the world operates on every level out of the patriarchal model that assumes male privilege and ownership of women. Male is the norm until or unless it is confronted, challenged and changed. Male heads of government rule. Educational systems live by male ways of imparting knowledge. Logic is valued above intuition. Medicine is dominated by male practitioners. The very ritual of weddings, symbolizes inequality in the relationship, and confers on the male certain "rights and controls" over women's bodies. Even in religion, supposedly a "sacred" domain, ordained of God, Priesthood and ministry are still often denied to women, and a male savior is required "to save us from our sins." Surely, my individual malaise and discontent were indeed universal. I was impacted to my very bones with the realization that there can be no peace without justice for women and girls.

I threw myself wholeheartedly into the Women's Liberation Movement, to learn as much as I could about what was going on with women worldwide as well as in America. I attended the United Nations Conferences on Women, held in 1980 in Mexico City, in 1985 in Kenya, Africa, and in 1990 in Beijing,

China. There I learned facts about the conditions with women and girls worldwide that shook me to the bone. I learned about rape being used as a bounty of war with so-called "comfort women" paying the price in bodily harm or even death. I learned again about girls as young as six being "given in marriage" to 60 year old men who use them as sex partners and slaves. I learned that 95% of the world's illiterates are girls and women. I learned that foot binding in China is NOT a thing of the past, that vaginal mutilation is still practiced as a religious ritual among many tribes and religions of the world. I learned that "cutting" is becoming more common in my own America as immigration brings in those of different religions and cultures. I learned that in many countries of the world, rape is considered a husband's "right," certainly not a crime or punishable by law. I learned that in the Congo a woman dies every minute in childbirth for lack of medical care. I learned that, after all our hard work in the seventies to change it, women in my rich America still earn only 77 cents to every dollar a man makes for the same work. (And Obama is ostracized for trying to get our do-nothing Congress to change that!) I learned that controlling the bodies and lives of women is going on all over the world. I became painfully aware of the Republican war on women at home in my own privileged America. The more I learned, the more astounded, enraged, and sad I became. I became more determined to dedicate my life to freeing women and girls for a better life. In any way I could. Wherever I could.

I would join women like Sheila Collins who wrote *A Different Heaven and Earth,* Merlin Stone who wrote *When God Was a Woman,* documenting an era when women were honored as priestesses and spiritual leaders—and then stamped out by a patriarchal "faith" that required "Thou shalt have no other God before me," the male Jahweh of the Christian religion.

I would write a book like *Beyond God the Father,* by Rosemary Reuther and John Bianchi. My book would document, as theirs did, emergence from worship of "The Heavenly Father" into the whole, freeing truth of God as Eternal, Creative Spirit, operative in women as well as men, dedicated to living in Love, Hope and Mystery. My book would be my personal declaration of faith.

At home in 2001 I joined an estimated 70,000 women from 182 countries in The World's March of Women, stopping traffic on the streets of New York from the United Nation's Building to the Statue of Liberty. On that march, *Sisterhood is Powerful,* the stirring book by Robin Morgan, became a visceral reality for me. It was heady stuff as we together embodied the injustices and inhumanities being committed against women in every town, country and byway of every nation. We joined hands across all borders of nations, races and creeds. We sang "We're on our way and we won't turn back." We screamed in our agony and determination, WOMEN OF THE WORLD UNITE! NO MORE VIOLENCE AGAINST WOMEN! The systems that deny our wholeness, body and soul, cannot stand. We are rising up to demand change. We will seek legislation to change unjust laws and reparations commensurate with the crimes against us.

We shouted slogans in all the languages on earth:

SISTERHOOD IS POWERFUL!

THINK GLOBALLY; ACT LOCALLY!

LISTEN TO WOMEN—FOR A CHANGE!

WE WANT JUSTICE! WE WANT PEACE!

ACT OUT THE PLATFORM! ACT ON IT NOW!

(The Women's Platform for Action was created and adopted at the UN Conference on Women in Beijing, China, in 1990.)

During that march, I saw with my own eyes how the courageous actions of an individual woman inspires other women to stand up and take the risks involved in saying "NO" to injustice and "YES" to change.

I immersed myself in protest marches. I read ever more widely. As a member of the Association for Creative Change, I attended its annual conferences. This kept me in touch with other social scientists who are committed to taking action to better women and girls' lives and the society at large.

As the wheels of time moved humanity into a new century, so I found myself as an individual woman entering a new era of my life journey, very new indeed. While every period of life presents new tasks, challenges and learnings, I knew the moment that October 2, 2001 rolled around, that this was different than all the days that had gone before. In so very many ways. I called it "My Numinous Nineties."

Nine

THE NUMINOUS NINETIES

Grow old along with me. The best is yet to be, the last of life, for which the first was made. Our times are in thy hands, who saith, 'The world I planned; be not afraid."[20]

According to Webster, numinous means "having a deeply spiritual or mystical effect. Divine." The great anthropologist and philosopher, Teilhard de Chardin once said: "We are not human beings on a spiritual journey; we are spiritual beings on a human journey." It makes all the difference in the world what your starting point is! If you believe you began life as the squalling tiny infant you were at birth, and that is all there is to you, you will approach aging and death as the end of everything. The Enemy!

Or, if on the other hand, you believe you are a free Spirit Essence that existed before, during, and after your short time and space-bound human form, you will approach aging and death as a doorway through which you step at death into a new reality beyond time and space, a Divine Essence.

I am now in my nineties, a time of great losses, like vision, hearing, and balance and a time of great gains like insight, wisdom and grandmothering. It is a time for more Being and less Doing. I speak now of my own lived nineties which I entered two years ago, the nineties which lead for most people, to the end of our human life on earth.

I entered my VERY OWN NINETIES a short time ago, short, but long enough for me to know that this age is different than any other I have ever lived through. Different in significant ways, notably, others' perceptions of me are quite unlike my own. I must look old and feeble, because I am either given great respect or conversely assumed to want and have no choice in matters that determine how I live. (Thankfully, this is *not* true of my children.) Tall men often run right into me and almost knock me down. I am now only 4 feet 11 inches, down from 5 feet 1 inch. Six-year olds and big dogs put me on alert. My softening muscles are no longer automatically dependable. They require daily attention at the Y to avoid the pain of old age's inevitable loss and change. Rarely a week goes by that does not find me in some doctor's office, or sometimes two or three. A broken tooth requires a filling. Shortness of breath demands increased use of inhalers. Trifocals no longer do the essential adjustments of focus. The age of Facebook, Twitter, Email, and Skype presents major challenges. I need help at the computer; I feel out of sync with my modern grandchildren. It is so much harder to stay in touch with them.

And then that long ago ditty comes to mind:
> *Your life depends on what you measure by;*
> *It's upward from the earth, or downward*
> *from the sky.*[21]

To which I added:
> *Your joy depends on your worldview,*
> *mindset;*
> *It's the many gifts YOU HAVE RECEIVED*
> *Or what you didn't get."*

My life is bountifully full these days. My children, their spouses and the grandchildren have opened a dozen new worlds for me: Music and Knitting (Eric and Jen), Elementary and Junior High School (Z Glenn and Arrow), Law (Bob and Joey), Urban Renewal (Danny), Psychology, (Jill), Medicine (Marta and Bart), Teach For America and Charter Schools (Tacey), Nursing (Emma), Travel (Grace, Cord, and Johnnie), AmeriCorps (Maria).

Girlfriends and boyfriends lurk around the edges of my life. Sarah and Tara, Cord and Joe. I can't even imagine how the turning of the seasons will expand the borders of the family, which is constantly changing.

I am standing in the doorway where two dimensions of life interact, and I know both are real. My task at this point is to keep both dimensions alive and well: this time-and-space-bound-human existence and the free Spirit Essence which so enriches our earthbound living even before death. In order to keep both alive, I have assigned myself several daily tasks.

SHAKE IT OUT
Experience the joy of movement by stretching.
First thing every morning, get rid of stiff joints and
encroaching arthritis. Practice right now. (Stand up,
stretch and shake.)

FEAST ON BEAUTY

Keep alive your soul's capacity for wonder —it's everywhere around you. A multitude of shades of green, tulips, daffodils, pink plum blossoms, white pear blossoms, oranges and the yellows of lemons, the pure white lilies for which the Bay Area is so famous. Take time to enjoy each one and all. Take a moment to marvel at the joy they bring. Hear the bluebird that trills from high on the telephone wire.

MOTHER YOURSELF

My 99-year old father often said: "Once a man and twice a child." Accept your limitations with the grace a child accepts the parents' care. Get the help you need to do whatever you need to do to stay alive and joyous.

MARVEL AT YOUR JOYS

Be happy that you can see, hear, and stay upright at least in this moment. Give thanks that you got out of bed on your own this morning.

BE SURPRISED AND SURPRISE SOMEBODY EVERY DAY

Who needs to hear your voice right now? Sing "Happy Birthday" to someone who doesn't expect it.

LEARN SOMETHING NEW EVERY DAY

Grow by tackling that computer glitch with new determination.

STAY CONNECTED
*Never let a day go by without talking with somebody
you love and haven't talked to for awhile.*

CATCH YOURSELF COMPLAINING
*Laugh a lot. Life is too short to spend it in regret
and fear*

GIVE YOURSELF AWAY
*Do a good deed every day for somebody having
a hard time.*

IN EVERYTHING GIVE THANKS
Find something good in the bad stuff

Above all, believe the poet Robert Browning, who once wrote:

"Grow old along with me. The best is yet to be, the last of life for which the first was made."[22]

I realized the truth of that this morning when I looked out my kitchen window into the fullness of chartreuse springtime. My very own Japanese maple swayed back and forth, yielding to gusty winds. It was as if the tree itself were dancing in glee at the return of its green life.

It is April, the time of the year when ongoing creation is rampant. Yesterday it was outrageously visible on my patio roof. Three squirrels were frisking about when two suddenly got serious and started making little squirrels while the third was determined to get into the act. One after another, the two males knocked each other off the female! It was a fun sight, an unexpected joy to watch in spite of the inner message I heard from long ago Mama on the farm: "If you come upon animals at each other, come away. Don't watch." I had no idea what she meant until one day when I came upon two sheep who were "at each other," and I didn't watch. Now in my 90's, I felt free to watch. To know and delight in creation in the making.

Nature is full of never ending marvelous surprises. To create or to enjoy watching creation is to live in the Spirit even though I am still in human form. Likewise, Memory has the power to bring joy, to transform my everyday living, to enable me to live in the Spirit beyond the confines of time and space.

Even in this very moment, memory places me back on that happy old Virginia farm. It is twilight, the hour of bird calls and low sight, a sense of the coming night. Cows bawl in the barnyard awaiting the coming milkers, all men, since "girls belong inside the house helping Mama." Daddy has spoken, and Daddy's word is the law of the family. Mama is preparing the evening meal for our fourteen: beef roast, the peck of potatoes I must peel to be mashed. And I must search the turkey field for the greens to go with them: poke, wild mustard, dandelion and Lamb's Quarter.

"Be careful to avoid the poisonous Jimsonweed." Daddy's admonition is fresh in my mind. I pick up the empty dishpan and head for the field. It doesn't take long to fill it, and I turn toward the kitchen.

On the doorstep I pause in the redolent air, as if listening for the beloved song of the whippoorwill. Sure enough, from the apple tree across the road and halfway down the lane where the cows meander toward the barnyard, there comes the lilting call: "Whippoorwill! Whippoorwill! All is well! All is well!" My girl voice mimics, "Whippoorwill! Whippoorwill!

Mama intervenes and breaks the mood: "Pick them over carefully and wash them three times before you put them on to cook." The old black, wood-burning range stands hot and ready.

Ninety years plus have gone by as a thief in the night, and I am no longer a child. Far, in another place and time, the warm evening air caresses me, and if I pay attention, in the far reaches of memory I hear the call:

Whippoorwill! Whippoorwill!
All is well! All is well.

Each and every one of my beloved grand-children and their parents continue to give me endless pride and joy. "Write for Your Life" is a constant, inspiration, a community of trust and care. My own creative life is still lively as I do good work on my memoirs.

The realm of Spirit is greatly enriched by, but not limited to memory. The first time I experienced this as real was when I was 14 or 15 years old in my youth group at Summit Church. We were hiking on Massanutten Peak for a vesper service: hiking through the dark woods for what seemed to me to be a long time, chattering all the way. Then, suddenly the path left the woods behind and emerged onto a wide space with a full view to the west, the sunset bathing the far Alleghenies in golden glory. I gasped; the group's chatter fell away into a hush; the Presence of God filled the silence. I knew as if for the first time in my life that this place was Holy Ground. Mystery and Wonder were not circumscribed by church walls. God was here and now, and I was one with the ongoing creation. That sense of continuing Presence stays with me still.

Years later I was alone at Sheep Creek Campground, where

King's Canyon and the High Sierras National Parks in California embody astounding, continuing creation. I had been alone, climbing and climbing the switchback trails, leading through the big trees to Land's End. At long last, the trail emerged onto a plateau, where open skies revealed row upon row of mountains nestling into each other, the blue Pacific on the far horizon. I breathed in the stunning beauty. And I had that sense of being beyond time and space, leaving my human body behind, the invisible becoming more real than the visible. My finite, human body freed from all limits, at one with all creation.

I now facilitate a writing group I call Write for Your Life. It has become a community of support and trust, peacemakers in this weary, war-torn world. Last February, after an especially moving session of deep sharing, I was feeling very connected to each one in the group. I left the church, walking toward my car to come home, and I suddenly saw just beyond a see-through veil, a beautiful vision of my loved ones, long gone and free, beckoning to me to join them in that spirit world. Then I realized that my heart was racing wildly, and I was near to dying. I heard myself saying, "Not yet. I have not finished writing my book."

Incredulously, I got in my car and drove to my doctor's office. "Beth, you don't have an appointment today," she said when she saw me.

"I know," I responded. "But there's something going on with my heart. Would you give a listen?"

She listened, agreed and sent me to get nitroglycerin at the drug store, and then home to bed. I did as she said; my heart settled down, and it's still beating. My doctor daughter called it malpractice.

Not all memories are peaceful; some are painfully poignant; all are sacred.

It is All Hallows' Eve, 1980. At home with Glenn.

"I guess we should head for the hospital Beth. This pain is getting worse." Fear grabbed at my insides, and I flew into action.

Flashing red lights and the screaming siren of the ambulance alerted the sleeping little village of Bridgewater that all was not well with one of its inhabitants. Neighbors in pajamas and nightgowns appeared on nearby porches and doorsteps openly, brazenly curious about what was going on. Inwardly I screamed, "Go back to your warm beds. It is not your life. It is only my loved one, and I in the grips of the inevitable, oncoming loss of my beloved."

An hour later, beside his bed, holding him lovingly, I felt the doctor's firm hand on my shoulders: "You must step outside now."

"I want to stay with him." The doctor pushed me out the door. I wandered the halls in shock and deep distress. A nurse saw me and asked, "Could I get you a glass of milk?"

"A cup of cold water would taste good." She brought it and I asked "What is your name?"

"My name is Rita."

"I will never forget you, Rita."

The biblical "cup of cold water" given in Christ's name flashed into my mind. It comforted me. I have never forgotten her. Sacred memory. Things of the Spirit. Nurturing still.

Not only memory activates the Spirit. I have time in the 90's for deep meditation and joy. Together with laughter, writing and grandmothering, I create worlds of healing and comfort.

Ten

THE UNFINISHED FEMINIST

*Never doubt that a small group of thoughtful,
committed citizens can change the world.
Indeed it's the only thing that ever has.*[23]

*Walk and move forward strongly.
Your futures are in front of you.*[24]

As I personally move deeper into the numinous nineties, the physical losses and restrictions of advancing old age slow me down, requiring new attention to time for exercise and sleep. At the same time, the miracles of technology speed up the flow of information worldwide, along with increased knowledge of far-flung issues, customs and religious rituals being experienced in the lives of girls and women. To say the least, I am horrified and shocked. There is abuse and injustice off the chart, everywhere.

Leaders of governments and nations are coping with violence and terrorism in increasing numbers. Television brings into our living rooms the reality of millions of displaced people, tribal killings, aggression on the part of tyrants in places of power. The planet seems to be shaking at the roots. Iraq, Iran,

Syria, Israel, the whole Middle East have become household names, our neighbors, threats to our national security.

I feel small and inconsequential, a tiny human organism among the seven plus billions of earth's humans. Yet, I am not without hope. I believe, as Margaret Mead said years ago: "Never doubt that a small group of thoughtful, committed citizens can change the world. Indeed it's the only thing that ever has."[25]

What I do matters. It will not be enough to bring peace with justice to the world in my lifetime, but I am doing what I can.

Nicholas Kristof and Sherryl WuDunn published a book in 2009 called *Half The Sky: Turning Oppression Into Opportunity For Women Worldwide.* That book shook me to the core, and left me with the fresh determination to spend the rest of my life empowering women and girls, wherever, whenever, and in any way that I can. Empowerment of women and girls, I realized, inevitably changes the lives of men and families for the better, making peace with justice possible in the world.

From that book I learned that every minute, somewhere in the world, a woman dies in childbirth. A girl is stoned to death in "an honor killing." In the world capital of rape in the eastern Congo, according to the UN, in remote villages, three-fourths of the women have endured savage torture and rape. Mass rapes have been reported at stunning levels during recent tribal and ethnic conflicts. Rings of prostitution damage or destroy the lives of girls worldwide. Brothels are "big business" all over the world. Genital mutilation (cutting) as a religious ritual is on the rise everywhere, including the US. Forty women every minute seek unsafe abortions.

In many developing countries, education for girls is considered to be a waste of time, so school for girls are mostly non-existent. Approximately 95 per cent of the illiterate of the world are female. Girls as young as six are married to, and become slaves of, sixty-year old men. These atrocities confront me everywhere I go: If I could live forever, I could not change them all.

The World Health Organization estimates that 536,000 women perished in pregnancy and childbirth in 2005, a toll that has barely budged in thirty years. Writers Kristof and WuDunn declare: "the oppression of women and girls around the globe is the central moral challenge of our time, the worst humanitarian crisis we face."

I live in an evil culture of gun violence, continuing injustice toward women worldwide, spying and drones, tyrants and incipient racism, abuse of power and deep fear and distrust of governments, nations and peoples. Terrorists worldwide set a tone of aggression and fear. The gap between the filthy rich and the abject poor create pockets of starving thousands in poverty and need.

At the same time, the human race is awakening to realize the responsibility and opportunity of changing that reality. Non-governmental organizations all over the world are springing up and taking action. I have belonged for almost 30 years to MADRE, meaning "mother" in Spanish. We work with women's groups in developing countries all over the world to connect those "haves" with poverty-stricken "have-nots," to raise the living standards of millions of families who live below the poverty level.

I belong to Heifer, International. We send live, pregnant animals to distraught people worldwide, people who are committed to sending the newborns on to their needy neighbors. Women for Women, International and Women's Empowerment International have joined the ranks of all these organizations who make micro-loans available to women who are starting small businesses. Their aim is to raise the standard of living for thousands of families in dire poverty in foreign countries, including the rich United States.

The present world is full of evil and danger; millions live in darkness and misery. The world is also full of dreams and visions, goodness and dedication to changing those realities. Humanity in all its complexity and fullness, its self-interest and greed, is moving toward the goal of wholeness for all, however slowly and painfully the journey evolves. For me, at this time of my life, I hear the agonizing moans of women all over the world caught in the horrors of injustice and abuse.

I am reminded of the great leader, Moses, who led his people out of oppression and slavery in Egypt and into forty years of wandering in the wilderness seeking freedom and justice. They endured all sorts of trials as they searched for the land "flowing with milk and honey." Finally, they climbed Mt. Nebo and got their first glimpse into that Promised Land. And Moses died there, having not reached his goal.

I call myself "the unfinished feminist."

I will not live to see my goal of peace and justice in the world, the outlawing of war and the coming of justice for women before I die, but I am still engaged in the journey toward it.

In 2001 I created (and still lead) two writing groups of mostly women who engage once a week in writing for spiritual growth and self-discovery. I belong and contribute regularly to "Women for Women, International" and "Empowerment of Women International." I contribute regularly to MADRE.

In my nineties there is so much I cannot do and there is so much I *can* do! I can support the groups that work to correct the horrendous injustice and abuse of women worldwide; I can speak for those whose voices are silenced: I can educate others to the situations of abject poverty and abuse that exist everywhere every day. More than a billion people in this world are living on less than $1.25 a day. Somewhere in the world, every nine seconds, a child dies from hunger.

Recently I was given the privilege of attending a workshop in snowy Maine. It was called "Sacred Journey." It was New Year's Day, 2013. The setting was a home full of windows, facing onto the banks of Union River near Ellsworth. Warm. Inviting. Privileged. Looking out on snow-laden pines, brilliant sun on piled high snow banks, beside plowed roads, the river moving serenely in the midst. A small group of women, pen and journal in hand, had been invited to a day of writing and reflection.

"Light a candle, and speak to what you take into the New Year," Sarah said.

En route by car to that home, I had been cogently reminded of mistakes I had made as a grandmother nine months previously. I was heavy, troubled with that knowledge which had come as a surprise to me. I lit a candle and said,

"I go into the New Year with a mixture of deep gratitude and deep regret: gratitude for the legacy of a strong family heritage and present support of loving family members; the goodness of life in its passage of seasons; regret over past mistakes, however unintended; robbery of my computer full of unbacked-up memoir writing, and with it the temporary loss of my sense of the worth of that writing at all; gratitude for a new computer and the will to start over."

"So what will the New Year bring for you?," asked Sarah. "There will be silence for writing. Take your lighted candle with you."

During that time, alone with my thoughts and dreams, I wrote:

"So—to the present Now. Gratitude and Wonder must win out in 2013. I resolve to start over again. I will put my writing at the top of my priority list, as an every day activity. I will write letters of regret asking for forgiveness of those who experienced hurt from me. I will do physical exercising every day in order to stay as mobile and flexible as I can. I will stay connected with my children, grandchildren and my "Write For Your Life" groups in order to feel nurtured in these aging years. I will feast on beauty and engage in Wonder, often. I will embrace the unknown—face whatever comes with calm acceptance—be at peace. In everything I will give thanks! I will rest in the Mystery of the realm of the Spirit and ongoing creation. I will call it all GOOD."

Then I wrote this little poem:

NEW YEAR'S DAY, 2013

A golden sun is traveling toward the snowy horizon.
A lone seagull flies westward;
A bevy of small black birds follows gaily along.

Lazy gold-rimmed clouds hang above the flowing river.
Serenity, silence, beauty prevail
In sure community.

New Year's Day 2013 is nearing its end
Leaving an open invitation
To take the blank pages of the sacred journal
And create the future
As I will.

I think the nineties of living are a time for *being, not doing,* learning to let doing be the activity of the young. A time to reflect and pay attention to things of the spirit.

This doesn't mean that I need not act when the ever-present hiddenness of misogyny rears its ugly head. This happened again on September 19, 2013. A friend shared with me her rage at her husband for his refusing to add her name to the will regarding their vacation home. I wrote her this letter:

I always get mad when women are mistreated. There are many ways that men abuse women, especially where money is concerned. Try this conversation on your husband:

Husband: My father gave me the money for that vacation home. You didn't pay a cent toward it and in the meantime, I paid all the bills because you didn't make enough to live on.

Wife: You paid half the bills. I paid the other half—in kind. If you paid me for the work I did to make you free to go to your work every day, I would have made three times as much. It's not my fault that women's work doesn't count for much in our society.

If I were to give you a bill it would look like this:

For Services Rendered (24 hours a day for umpteen years)
Childcare Provider—double for the disabled one—?
Teacher—?
Chauffeur on Notice—?
Laundress for the whole family—?
House cleaner and General Housekeeper—?
Grocery Shopper—?
Cook—?
Doctor and Comforter—?
Miscellaneous, on Call—?

Wife: You do the numbers and add my name to the vacation home on your will. No more belittling my work. I want to be appreciated.

No arguments, L. Stay clear and firm. Stick up for your rights!

Courage, Beth

L. later told me the letter really helped her in her conversation with her husband.

This kind of help for women gives me hope for the future of women and girls.

Memories are things of the spirit. October 24, 1952, red letter day of my advent into motherhood, the hoped for fulfillment of my dream. Autumn dressed to the hilt. A flaming maple just outside the window of the maternity ward in Roaring Spring, in a blazing Pennsylvania fall. Moans of a womb giving birth for the first time. Then. A new voice from a 9-pound hunk of red-haired humanity squalling to the outside air, "I am here!

Look at me!" Red-gold reflection of the burning tree, here with all her embryonic hopes and dreams, fragile arms and legs rippling the air to join in the broody dance of life. Singing the age-old song of birth: "I am here! Look at me!"

"I see you, precious daughter. Your name is Peggy Ruth," I said in answer.

For 19 too short years she danced—and then, was gone.

October 24, 2012. California in reds, yellows, golds and bronze, old dry greens leaves blowing in the wind, turning trees into black lace. The time of ghoulies and ghosts, witches riding brooms, children turned into sagging, make-believe giraffes, lions, tigers and electric lightbulbs, roaming the streets calling "Trick or Treat." And in the midst, that spirit voice of Peggy crying, "Mother, I am here. Look at me! I have come in Spirit form to remind you of the love and goodness I brought the first time I came. The joys that tumbled one upon another in those 19 years. The music, laughter, tears and growing-up struggles. Above all, your infinite belief in my possibilities. Our race for the Ph D. You won. But I am still here, Mother. Remember me and be glad."

And I do remember and am glad.

And my heart aches.

Memories are things of the spirit.

I am well aware that my human lifetime is limited in time and energy.

I hear myself singing in the words of the plaintive spiritual: "This world is not my home; I'm just a-passin' through.... If heaven's not my home, Then Lord what shall I do? The angels beckon me from heaven's open door. And I can't feel at home in this world anymore."[26]

I have a favorite Bible verse—Jesus is praising a woman who anointed him with an expensive ointment of *nard*. He said to heckling men: "Leave her alone.... She has done what she could."[27]

I have done what I could to be faithful to the vision. The world is awakening slowly but surely to the plight of women and girls. The task of liberating them remains unfinished; and I with them, the unfinished feminist.

As I stand on the threshold of new dimensions beyond the human limitations of time and space, I face into the task of letting go much of the *doing* of past years.

I hear the poet calling:

Hold high the torch!
You did not light its glow.
'Twas given you by others' hands, you know.
'Twas yours awhile to keep it burning bright.
 But MILLIONS STILL in darkness
Moan and WEEP for light.
Pass on the torch!
You did not light its glow.
'Twas given you by other hands, you know.[28]

When my human race is run, let it be said of me as of Mary Magdalene, "She has done what she could."[29]

APPENDIX A

Peggy, I May Not Have The Summer,
by Beth Glick-Rieman
Copyright 2010

Chapter 1: Oh Peggy, My Peggy

Speaking of the death of the young, Viktor Frankl said:
"We cannot, after all, judge a biography by its length,
by the number of pages in; we must judge by the
richness of the contents. ...Sometimes the 'unfinished'
are among the most beautiful symphonies.[30]

...It is Spring somewhere
every time a Little Girl is born.[31]

It was Spring in the golden October of Pennsylvania the day Peggy was born. The spreading maple tree outside my hospital window was aflame with reds and golds, as if to announce a major changing of seasons. I had not the faintest conception of how far-reaching that change would be for me and the family...

For five long years before Peggy's birth, Glenn and I had longed for a child and finally had begun the process of adoption. Then I got pregnant. The moment of Peggy's healthy birth was a time of awe and wonder. It was 1952. At the end of those long seven days in the hospital, I found it strangely hard to believe that this tiny, marvelous human being was really ours, and we could take her home to live with us. She seemed to me to be a miracle from the start, a squalling bit of humanity entrusted to our care.

Peggy was born into a loving and stable family. Before we married, Glenn and I had long talks about the kind of marriage we wanted to have and the kind of parents we wanted to be. We had agreed that our guiding principle with each other and any children who would join us would be profound respect for one another. We would be loving, kind, and generous in praise. In our young idealism, we wanted to be the best parents in the whole world.

It goes without saying that in real life we were not always able to live up to our expectations of ourselves. In those days, our very understanding of being "good parents" included a double standard between parents and children. We accepted as true and uncontestable fact that the balance of power was unequal from the start. We parents "knew what was best", and we would make the final decisions about what was right for the family. At the same time, we sincerely wanted each child to know that what they felt was important to us, and we would pay attention to their frustrations, angers and wants because they really mattered to us. Over the years, we learned as parents to regret our mistakes, to apologize for our failures and to ask for forgiveness

Glenn and I both loved books, art, music and travel. He had a wry sense of humor. Laughter was no stranger to our family's life. On the other hand, we had both inherited the Protestant work ethic. My mother's injunction, which often rang in my ears, was handed down to my own children: "Idle hands are the devil's workshop." We wanted the children to keep busy, to do their part with chores, to make a contribution to the work needed to keep the family functioning well. We also wanted them to have a voice in the decisions that affected them.

We created what we called "Family Council." Once a week everyone was expected to meet together to create the "Chore Chart" for that week. These charts were posted on a bulletin board in the kitchen to remind all of us what our tasks were for that week. Family Council was a time for each child, and also the parents, to talk about any grievances we had about what had happened during the week and what we wanted to discuss or have changed. We took the children seriously. We listened and made changes to meet their needs whenever possible. I smile as I remember how intense these times became and how seriously we all considered them. Looking back on those meetings, I realize how important they were to the feeling of solidarity in the family. We learned a lot about what was going on in the children's lives and what struggles they were having. When it was not possible to do as they wished, we made it our task to help them understand why we felt it was important to make the decisions that we made.

Peggy, as the oldest of five children, was self-motivated, an initiator with a commanding presence in the family circle. She was often dominating in her manner, demanding and did not take kindly to our comments that she learn to be more thoughtful of others' needs and wants. From early childhood, she was not one to live by others' rules or wants, a trait that sometimes created conflict between herself and her siblings and parents. At age two or so, she would hide her favorite toys when she knew other children would be visiting. At age four, when she saw me teaching the students that came to the house for piano lessons, she decided that she wanted to learn to play the piano. She begged with such insistence that I started to give her lessons. I can still see her standing on tiptoe to reach the keys to practice. I never had to remind her.

When I think of the child Peggy now, in my mind's eye, I see a red-headed toddler with one of her favorite books, "Julie and her Nine Friendly Dogs." Seventeen months old, and she is "reading" while she potty-trains herself. Impatiently, she corrects my faulty memory as I "tell" the story and wash the dishes at the sink on the other side of the room. Two short years later, she spells out the "hard words" as she takes to reading as a duck to water.

One very special gift we received at the time of her birth was a book written by Louis Redmond. It was called *What I Know About Girls*. I treasured that book then, and I still do today. Redmond did indeed know about girls. It was as if he were talking about Peggy when he wrote:

The face of a Little Girl reading is like a deep, quiet pool you find in the woods, which receives in its stillness all the wonders of the wide, clean sky. Cloud-people wander there, and birds pass, and sunlight twinkles, while the noisy real world stands at a respectful distance.[32]

When Peggy was reading, she was not present. She was "somewhere else."

A week after Peggy died, I received a letter from my sister. It painted this picture of our beloved child:

Somewhere a bird is twittering, and I remember little Peggy —only a couple of years old, going with Aunt Mickie to the pig pen on Granddaddy's farm to see the pigs—stop and pull my hand and say, 'Hear the birds sing, Aunt Mickie!' She was full of wonder at age 3 or 4. She made so much music of her own—she brought so much joy to you two as well as to others as she grew. I loved your child Peggy —long before I had my own children to love. I loved her because she was born to people I loved, because of her brightness, her sensitivity, her music. She was always special to me, I think partly because she was so special to you, and I know how deeply she was wanted and welcomed and how great the joy her coming brought.

It must be a least several years now since I have seen Peggy. My children remember her very little. They know I am sad; they ask for little things to identify what she was like. I talk of her violin, her red hair, her sensitivity, and of how deeply she was loved. And I am sorry they will never know Peggy, for I am better for having had that opportunity.

As a child, Peggy was a tree climber. When I could not find her and she did not answer my calling, I would look in her favorite tree where she was often lost in the world of words, ideas and wonderings. The teenager Peggy always had a book in her hands. Her alert and fertile mind traveled the globe, drinking in knowledge at every opportunity, always reaching for understanding of her world, determined to be involved in making it better.

She early defined for herself what was right for her to do and stubbornly held to those definitions. Near the end of her first year in college she wrote us a letter that shook my moral codes to the foundations. In it she said she wanted to come home for particular weekend, and she was bringing John. And, "Just so you know, we will be sleeping together. If you and Daddy can't permit that to happen, then John will not come, and neither will I!" That news shocked us in more ways than one, and created for me a profound moral dilemma. My moral code then did not allow for sex before marriage, and with three siblings younger than she, taking their cues from her, I did not want that example set for them.

When Glenn and I talked about how to respond, my initial response was a loud "NO! When she is in our house, she needs to live by our rules."

Glenn was wiser, not so rigid.

"Beth, don't you think that our relationship with Peggy is more important than her living by our moral codes of conduct? If we say no to this, we will be driving a wedge between us." I had to agree, and we had a wonderful weekend together learning to love Peggy as a young adult and this John who had gained her love.

It was the summer just before she was nineteen, that the headstrong, willful Peggy gave us a scare that still gives me chills. She was living at home, working in the local library in Dayton, Ohio, also John's hometown. One night she asked for the van to go and spend the evening with him. She assured us she'd be back no later than 11:00. She was not back at 11:00. Or 12:00. We became anxious, called John's home and learned that he had left her at 10:00. They had met in a park; then had broken up and when he left, she was quite upset. We asked him to go back to that spot to see if she was still there. He called back to say the van was gone, and there was no sign of her anywhere.

We agonized over what to do. We could alert the police, though that did not seem right for Peggy. It might cause her embarrassment or worse, to have an accident and hurt herself. But what alternative was there? Where might she have gone? We imagined one place after another; none seemed to be right. Then, at about 2:00 AM it suddenly occurred to me that she might have driven back to the college four hours away to talk with her last year's roommate who was there for the summer. Glenn's brother lived in that town. We called him out of bed, asked if he would drive over to the house where her roommate lived, and see if the van was there. Not to do anything, but just to call us back and let us know. The van was there, and the lights were on in the house. We asked him to make a call to her, to tell her that we loved her and wanted her to come home. It was 3:00 AM. A half hour later he called back to tell us, "She says she will come home tomorrow."

We went to bed and slept fitfully. The next morning I prepared a picnic with Peggy's favorite foods—fried chicken, potato salad, baked beans. Glenn worked in the yard mowing, in the garden staking up tomatoes. Our hands busy; our minds were on the empty driveway. The day dragged by. Our relief of the night before was swallowed up in tension and anxiety. Her siblings were subdued, doing their chores without argument, as if they did not want to add to our anxiety. At dusk, we gathered around the picnic table to watch and wait.

We waited and waited and waited. Then, the sound of a motor; the van appeared in the driveway. It was 6:30 in the evening. I broke into tears of relief. Glenn got up, pulled a pair of scissors out of his pocket, walked over to a blooming red rose bush and cut a long stem rose. As Peggy started across the lawn toward us, he walked to her, gave her the rose, and without a word, took her in his arms in a strong embrace. My hug was next, and the family chatter began ever so naturally. Our Peggy was safely back in the family circle.

Peggy lived a lot of years in her short nineteen. She never did one thing at a time. Homework and music went together. While writing a term paper, she made a dress for the prom. By the time she was in her teens, she had learned to sew, do macramé, play the piano and guitar, sing, be a friend to a lot of people, make top grades in her school work. By the time she was nineteen, she had become a feminist, a protester for peace, a college student of two years, a traveler to Mexico with some speaking knowledge of Spanish, a lover, a poet and writer, an adventurer in nature, a debater, a champion for justice, a philosopher.

She had written about death and its meaning and had made a will. She continued to amaze us, this girl. Until she was ten years old, we had no boy children, so we assumed that Redmond was right, when he spoke of the difference between boys and girls:

A boy, being earth-bound, must get off his bicycle before he can climb into a tree. But a little girl can fly with the robin to her nest while pedaling rapidly down the street"[33]

Peggy was a high-energy person. She did not want to waste one moment. In a way that I will never understand, she knew beyond her years that life is precious and fleeting. From the time she was twelve she commented: "I don't have much time. I will die young." Her robust young health belied the words, but the comment troubled me. She seemed to say it, not out of a morbid fascination with death, but rather as a matter of fact, something she knew that was hidden to me.

In death, she left behind a stack of creative writings that painted for us a picture of what she thought about herself and the kind of person she believed herself to be. She wrote this poem to her lover the year before she died:

if you like girls
who swing on swings
and wade in brooks
and revel in the smell of spring
then stay awhile.

if you like girls whose hearts are light
and as a child's
and still their minds are clear and bright
then stay a while.

if you like girls
who love the way
you walk and talk
and miss you when you've gone away
then stay a while.

if you like girls
when they kiss you
and when they laugh
and even when they're sad and blue
oh...please stay a while.

> *but if you don't believe*
> *in flying kites*
> *and riding bikes*
> *and loving me like i love you*
> *then leave me now –*
> *before my heart*
> *is too full of what you are*
> *to let you go.*

On her desk, dated May 11, 1972, the day before the accident and nine days before her death, there was a fragment of a journal entry:

> *Now politics is becoming more & more integrated into my life & is almost indistinguishable from so-called "personal problems." My priorities have changed for the better.... I've decided that in times of crisis I have to act w/what can be quickly mobilized, & spend the quieter times building a base in town. Also, it is very important for women to be in leadership positions.... I've come to believe there's no time to be wasted.*

Alongside the journal entry, there was a self-assigned list for summer learning. She had set for herself the task of "reading two hours daily, economic theory, more work on China, and the history of the Paris Commune, the German putsches and the Russian Revolution, organizing town halls, maybe free school, or a series of public debates."

The year before she died a friend of hers was struggling with the question of death and Peggy wrote this letter to her:

The whole point of life is change, radical change, and characteristic is our resistance to that change. I don't know, but I bet I even resisted being born, and as it turned out that was the best thing that ever happened to me. I thought the world was going to end when we moved from Pennsylvania to Ohio, but somehow I made it and was glad for it. With every relationship I've had that became altered, I was sure it would never be good again and that nothing could replace it. But somehow it always is good, never in the same way as before, but always in new and exciting ways. The end is never good in itself, just for what it brings.... that's strange about life—for all that we think we know what makes us happy, we can never at any point say, "Here is where I want to stay," because that is to deny possibility. Sometimes we set standards of goodness— we say, "If only she could stay three forever" and stuff like that. That's pointless; we shouldn't cling in the face of inevitability but welcome the progress. It's all part of a growth process and we should always, always seek to grow. I think that process is continuous. Maybe even death is like a pause to flip the record so we can hear the other side.

For me, I want to go in the middle of something going on—none of this lingering around stuff. I know some people want time to prepare, but I don't see the point. Why waste time thinking about it? Death should happen like life does—right in the middle of happenings. If we concentrate on immediate life, it should be enough to have had good times and good friends, and as little regret as possible. There's no better way to die.

The hardest thing about a premature death is the realization that to us they are no longer becoming, but become. Remember when we read Bonheoffer? Letters and Papers from Prison *makes us aware of what he might have become had he lived; at the same time it points out that what he did in his relatively short life was so urgently important. He had no time to waste, and we have no time to waste reflecting on what can't be. His potential becomes ours, and we must work from there.*

It was on the Tuesday before her death that her doctor had confronted her about a poster on her wall. There was a significant change in the care he gave her after that, not even seeing her on daily rounds. What he had said when I protested to him about that, are words burned into my memory: "I'm taking care of a lot of old people who don't have long to live. She has her whole life ahead of her." Her "whole life" was three days. She paid the awful price of his negligence with her life.

"Death should happen like life does," she had said, "right in the middle of happenings." And so it did. Peggy got her wish. She died right in the midst of "happenings." Her exams at college would have started the next week, moving her toward the completion of her sophomore year.

Spring was on the threshold and the Lilies-of-the-Valley she loved so well were just beginning to bloom.

"I'm missing Spring, Mother," she had wailed from her hospital bed two days earlier. Peggy was cut down in the prime of her life, right in the midst of her hopes and dreams for the future. And mine.

As I walked into her room in the early morning on the day she died, her words hit like a hammer. "I am dying today Mother. Don't punish yourself in grieving. And don't call me a rose. I've been a pain lots of times. So let my life be what it was and then move on."

In the darkness of early evening, as the blood clot hit her lung, the walls of that hospital room vibrated with her heart-rending scream, "MOTHER!" It was her last word.

Or was it, really? It was like Peggy not to give up hope. As I stood alone in complete shock by the bedside where she lay in death, a note on her nightstand flashed into my vision. I picked it up. It was written in a very shaky hand, so unlike the fluid clarity of her writing. It must have taken superhuman effort to write to a dear friend, as the fatal blood clot traveled on its way.

I picked up the note and read it through the first of oceans of tears. I saw in her words her fears, her anguish, and her will to live. I read:

Dear Rock:

I am in pain and very weak: I find
reading & thinking hard. I have surgery
again Wednesday which will wipe me out
even more. They think I may have spinal
damage, too. But I am fighting to get
well & out of here. The best way to
fight seems to be by resting, so that's

what I mostly do. Traction is a pain.
Your letter was fine—sorry I can't
Answer in kind. My friends are so good.
Vencero (I shall triumph)
   Peg

Her very last word was a word of Spirit and Hope: *Vencero!*
Venceremos, my Peggy. We shall triumph. The road will be long and hard, but your courage will strengthen our hearts. You said, "Let my life be what it was and then move on." You said you had no time to waste, that your potential becomes ours and we must work from there. And so it is.

Yet even now, thirty-eight years later, deep in my soul I grieve your loss. The eight days of your dying were a cosmic shock that changed by life forever.

Going to the Roots
A Sermon Preached by Beth Glick-Rieman
Christ Church
Edinburgh, Scotland
October 10, 1993

It is more than a pleasure for me to be here today—it seems like something of a miracle. Never in my wildest imaginings as a child when I sang with such fervor, "On yon bonnie banks and on yon bonnie braes, where the sun shines bright on Loch Lomond" would I have dreamed that I would one day stand in this sacred place with real, honest-to-goodness Scots listening to what I have to say! But here I am, and very privileged to be with you.

At home I am considered by some to be a "radical feminist theologian," and it is out of my life experience which has prompted that description that I want to share with you today. Feminism for me is a justice issue—not at all confined to women, but is inclusive of everyone. It has to do with the Old Testament understanding of righteousness as living in right relationship with others. It stands in sharp contrast to "patriarchy," which I define as a prevailing system of dominance and submission. The word, "radical" means "of or from the roots—going to the foundation or source of something."

As I go to the roots of my own spiritual journey, I find there three feminist principles that guide my life. The first is: empowerment; the second is mutuality; the third is interdependence, the interconnection of all living things. I want to share with you what these mean to me, as they are found in our three Bible passages of this day. The common thread among these passages is the element of CHOICE.

Let us look at the first—empowerment—not power over, but power with. Our societies are organized around "power over." There is the "top," the person in charge who makes the decisions that affect the rest of us, and there is the "bottom," the disenfranchised and marginal people who are often poor and in need, victims of greed, war and selfish pleasures on the part of the "haves." Then there is the "middle" in terms we sometimes have power and sometimes don't. I would guess that a lot of us here feel that's where we are.

In the story of Moses we heard today, we have a powerful example of "power with." He could look over into the Promised Land, but he would die before he reached there. Like Moses, we live in a time of change and struggle. We can see with our inner eyes of vision the Promised Land of a church beyond the issues of gender, truly committed to change for the sake of the well-being of all. And we can work for and hope for its coming. The truth is, it will probably not be achieved in our lifetime. Can you imagine yourself, for example, being able to include Mother as well as Father when you speak of the mystery of Divine Holiness at the heart of Creation? Like Moses, we have a choice: we can work toward that Promised Land of a time beyond the elevation of one sex over another— or we can be bitter about that and give up hope. But look at that powerful little story at the time of Moses' death. Right in the middle of the extolling of his great leadership and his face to face relationship with God, we read these words: "And Joshua, the son of Nun was full of the spirit of wisdom, for Moses had laid his hands upon him." What Moses could not do, he empowered someone else to do. He called out the gifts of the one who *would* lead the people into the Promised Land. This is a remarkable story of EMPOWERMENT.

In my struggle to live the good life, I know that empowering others is a divine calling, for I myself have been empowered by others, and I know what that can mean in calling out my gifts. My very being here is an example of empowerment—the miracle of being valued, of being seen as having some wisdom to share. That is a great gift.

Someone, somewhere is needing *you* to believe in them, to lay hands on them, to empower them to become more than they ever thought they could be. If that happens, it will be because you *choose* to do it.

The second principle—MUTUALITY. Equality. Sharing in common, having equal access to resources, decision-making, privilege, each one being recognized as of as much value as any other.

Our gospel lesson of today has troubled me over many years. Today I know it is because for me it is an example of the lack of mutuality. It seems to be saying "come to the feast" and then "You are not acceptable. Get Out!" My own very personal experience as a lifelong member of the church resonates with that. Long years ago, when I was about eight years old, I sat with my farmer father on a low wall of an old wagon shed. He asked me, "What do you want to be when you grow up,

Elizabeth?" I answered: "A preacher like you, Daddy." There was a long pause. Then he said, "You're a girl. You could be a missionary or a Christian educator." Always before he had said, "You can be anything you want to be." The message I received resonates with the gospel story. "Come to the feast—but you are not acceptable as you are." It hurt all the more because I could not change being "a girl." It often hurts today still because I cannot change being a woman, and seeing the church through my own woman experience.

What was the "wedding garment" which was unacceptable? I do not know what it was for the person in the story. I do know that, for me, it was an accident of my birth. It was the opposite of empowerment. It took me almost fifty years to realize that Daddy was caught in his own understanding of male/female roles in the church and that my calling was indeed to the ordained ministry.

In this story there is no sense of mutuality. The king is in charge—he has the resources to put on a feast; he has the right to decide who is in and who is out; he has the power to exclude. His choices determine whether someone is acceptable or not. The story ends with "many are called, but few are chosen."

Many times in my life in the church, I feel called, but not chosen. Just two weeks ago at a meeting in Chicago, I felt valued when I was asked by a Roman Catholic priest to work with a Protestant sister to lead a service of worship and communion. We had chosen to use bread and water, the elements of common life, without which we cannot live. As we gathered for the services, the priest, whom I love as a brother, asked, "Where is the wine?" And I responded, "We can live without wine, but not water."

The message was: this is not the REAL commemoration of Christ's passion. In my heart, I felt the judgment that I was not quite acceptable, that my experience was somehow devalued, that I was called, but not chosen.

Who are the "kings" in the life of the church today? How can we move toward mutuality—being open to and valuing all perspectives and gifts as of equal worth, even those with whom we disagree? What do you need to do to break down the walls of privilege and inequality and judgment? Where can you champion the cause of someone who is devalued?

The third principle that is central in my spiritual understandings is INTERDEPENDENCE, INTERCONNECTION. This includes not only the human family, but also the planet which is the source of our life. To live by this principle requires the choices to be transformed, to see life differently and to behave out of that new vision. That is not easy in a world where people assume that what they have been taught is the only or right way to live.

That was Paul's challenge to Philemon, the slave-owner. Owning slaves was a practice fully accepted in that day. But Philemon must have been a hard master, for Onesimus ran away, apparently to seek from Paul some comfort and support. Look at what Paul did. Out of respect for Philemon, he sent Onesimus back. But not without giving Philemon a hard choice to change the way he saw the master/ slave relationship. He wrote him a letter saying, "Onesimus left as a slave. I return him to you as a brother. Formerly he was useless. Now he is useful. I am sending him back to you sending my very heart." Onesimus' very life depended on Philemon's choice to undergo radical transformation, to be open to seeing himself as interconnected with Onesimus as a brother. Philemon was the one in power. He could make a difference—he could live by the principle of interdependence and break down the barriers of owner/ slave. To do that, he would need from that point on to see Onesimus, not as that which he owned, but as a member of his own family.

It was in his everyday contacts that Jesus confronted the injustices of his day, and he paid for it with his life. He broke down the barriers of race by speaking to a Samaritan woman of a hated race. He broke down the double standard between men and women when he said to the men about to stone the woman, "Which of *you* is guilty? She could not commit adultery alone." On the cross, he broke down the narrow definitions of family. He said, "All of these are my brothers and sisters." Jesus loved and respected the earth. He said, "Consider the lilies of the field." Consider the environment on which we all depend for life. We are all one. What hurts the Mother Earth or anyone in it hurts us all. The polluted air and water of the United Sates affects the quality of life in Scotland. We are interdependent, and we need each other to be whole.

Many women are leaving the church today. Are they the run-away slaves who seek the Promised Land of a larger freedom, wholeness and inclusion as full members of the family of the faithful?

I close with Paul's words to Philemon: "though I am bold enough in Christ to command you to do what is required, yet for love's sake I prefer to appeal to you." Today, my friends, I make *my* appeal to you in the name of love and in the fullness of my heart.

We have all been given a choice. How will we respond?

Let us pray.

O Great Spirit of love and creative power, move in us and among us to heal our brokenness. Move us to empowerment of ourselves and others so that we may live in genuine mutuality. Help us to keep clear the vision of the Promised Land where we live out true interconnection and interdependence. Open our eyes to see the choices we can make to move us toward that vision.

In the name of the Christ of love we pray. Amen.

She Has Done What She Could

No Peace Without Justice

ENDNOTES

1. *The Bible,* Exodus 20:1–17.

2. *The Bible,* Psalms 24:1.

3. "Playing With Time" WFYL. Baker, p. 102.

4. "The Chrysalis Effect" pp. 29–32 Sussex Academic Press, 2009.

5. Martin Luther King, Jr., *Where Do We Go from Here: Chaos or Community?,* pp. 62–63, 1967.

6. *An Almanac for the Soul,* Mary and Nancy Hiles.

7. J.R.R. Tolkein, *The Fellowship of the Ring.* Del Rey: Reissue Edition, August 12, 1986.

8. The Second Himalayan Expedition, W.H. Murray, quoting Goethe.

9. Albert Einstein.

10. John 8:32. *The Holy Bible,* Revised Standard Version. New York: Thomas Nelson & Sons, Old Testament Section, 1952, New Testament Section, 1946.

11. John 8:32. *The Holy Bible,* Revised Standard Version. New York: Thomas Nelson & Sons, Old Testament Section, 1952, New Testament Section, 1946.

12. Martin Luther King, Jr. Speech: "A Proper Sense of Priorities," February 6, 1968, Washington, D.C.

13. *The Bible,* Matthew 5:4.

14. *The Holy Bible,* Revised Standard Version.

15. *The Holy Bible,* Revised Standard Version.

16. *The Holy Bible,* Revised Standard Version.

17. *The Holy Bible,* Revised Standard Version.

18. *The Holy Bible,* Revised Standard Version.

19. "The Denial of Death" by Ernest Becker p. 74 in *Almanac for the Soul* ed. Hiles.

20. "Rabbi Ben Ezra," a poem by Robert Browning.

21. Anonymous.

22. "Rabbi Ben Ezra," a poem by Robert Browning.

23. Attributed to Margaret Mead.

24. Phuong Giang, librarian, Ngu Hiep #I Primary School, Tien Giang Province, Vietnam. As quoted in *Creating Room to Read: A Story of Hope in the Battle for Global Literacy*, by John Wood. Plume, Published by the Penguin Group, New York, 2013.

25. Attributed to Margaret Mead.

26. *This World is Not My Home*, Recorded by Jim Reeves, written by Mary Reeves and Albert E. Brumley.

27. *The Bible,* Mark 14: 8-9.

28. Anonymous.

29. *The Bible,* Mark 14:8.

30. Tatelbaum, Judy. Perennial Library, Harper & Row, New York, 1980 p. 14

31 Redmond, Louis, What I Know About Girls, Hanover House, Garden City, NY, 1952 p. 21

32. Redmond, Ibid. p. 24

33. Redmond, Ibid. p. 13

20571284R00127

Made in the USA
San Bernardino, CA
16 April 2015